PROMOTION OF THE RIGHTS OF PATIENTS IN EUROPE

Promotion of the Rights of Patients in Europe

Proceedings of a WHO Consultation

Published on behalf of the
World Health Organization, Regional Office for Europe
in collaboration with the
Health Law Section, University of Amsterdam

Kluwer Law International
The Hague / London / Boston

A C.I.P. Catalogue record for this book is available from the Library of Congress.

ISBN 90-411-0100-4

Published by Kluwer Law International,
P.O. Box 85889, 2508 CN The Hague, The Netherlands.

Sold and distributed in the U.S.A. and Canada
by Kluwer Law International,
675 Massachusetts Avenue, Cambridge, MA 02139, U.S.A.

In all other countries, sold and distributed
by Kluwer Law International,
P.O. Box 322, 3300 AH Dordrecht, The Netherlands.

The views expressed in this publication are those of the authors and do not necessarily represent the decisions or the stated policy of the World Health Organization.

Printed on acid-free paper

Kluwer Law International incorporates the publishing programmes of
Graham & Trotman Ltd, Kluwer Law and Taxation Publishers,
and Martinus Nijhoff Publishers.

Printed in the Netherlands

Contents

Part IV. Understanding the Challenges

Part V. The Netherlands Experience

Part VI. Where Do We Go from Here?

Foreword

During the last decades there has been a progressive acceptance of human rights as expressed in United Nations human rights instruments and those of the Council of Europe. One of its effects has been a very positive international trend in the consideration and definition of patients' rights. In the WHO European Region, the trend has been influenced by a number of changes in the health sector. These are most notably the emergence of new ethical issues, which are a direct consequence of progress in biomedical science and technology, and particularly in the many new Member States, the rapid, radical change in the social, political, and economic environments, which is shaping the health care reform process in countries.

Through the 1980s, studies and surveys revealed a number of policy trends and normative initiatives in countries. The most recent study results were published in the book *The rights of patients in Europe*.[1] With such evidence establishing the common interest, it became increasingly clear that additional support to policy development in many of those countries would now be appropriate.

With the support of the Government of the Netherlands and in consultation with governments and other interested parties in countries, a group of technical experts convened by the health legislation unit of the WHO Regional Office for Europe drafted a comprehensive basic guidance

[1] LEENEN, H. ET AL. *The rights of patients in Europe*. Deventer, Kluwer Law and Taxation Publishers, 1993.

document *Principles of the rights of patients in Europe* (see Chapter 4). Their objective was to produce a text that the responsible bodies within countries could put to practical use according to their needs and circumstances. I believe that the expert group succeeded admirably.

We have come to the end of a long preparatory process during which the Regional Office has given sustained encouragement to the emerging patients' rights movement. The 1994 European Consultation on the Rights of Patients, convened under the auspices of the WHO Regional Office, hosted by the Government of the Netherlands and attended by representatives from 36 Member States, had a very deliberate purpose. It was to define principles and strategies for promoting the rights of patients within the context of the health care reform process.

In addition to the guidance document, which was presented and commended by the distinguished chair of the expert group, Professor Leenen, the Consultation had the benefit of a series of authoritative briefings from members of the drafting group and leading representatives of various physician, patient, and citizens organizations, as well as from the Council of Europe, a sister international organization that has done pioneering work in the field of rights. We particularly welcomed the two insightful and complementary presentations of the Netherlands Medical Association and Consumer Organization as an inspirational example of what could be accomplished when there is a will to work together for a common cause.

Another notable feature of the Consultation was the way it placed patients' rights in the context and perspective of other significant emergent trends and issues: patient education and health education, provider–patient relationships, and social rights and citizens' views on health care reforms.

We cannot underestimate the power of these developments to change the direction and culture of health care that we have known so far as the era of modern medicine. Patient education has the potential to transform the role of the patient. It seeks to empower patients as participants in, rather than passive recipients of, their care and treatment. With their diagnoses properly explained to them, they participate in the consideration of the risks and benefits of possible treatment options. Conscious of their rights, they understand their responsibilities for their own health.

The relationship between the provider and receiver of care is critical to the realization of the concept of partnership in care. Its success hinges in large measure on the provider's understanding of the patient's rights and role in the relationship. Training for health personnel in provider–patient relationships becomes an essential element in any patients' rights strategy.

But reforming relationships within the care process, though essential, is not enough. There must be free and effective dissemination of information about the causes and prevention of disease and disability, and about the protection and promotion of health. There must be proper and universally available skills training to enable people to use that information to care for themselves and maintain their health. These are necessary tasks of health education.

The goal of social rights is the goal of equity, to ensure the fullest participation of all people in society. In terms of health, these social rights are most frequently related to the right to health care, with an emphasis on equity, which is of course the foundation of the WHO health for all strategy. This brings us to the heart of the current debate over health care reform in many European Member States. It reflects the search for effective, equitable and politically viable methods of financing health care, as well as equity of access to care and equity in the outcome and quality of care. The importance given to citizens' views in these debates is a revealing indicator of the strength of participatory democracy in our societies. A democracy marked by strong, active citizen participation, in which the voice of the citizen is listened to by policy- and decision-makers, is one in which patients' rights will not merely be formally implemented but truly observed in daily practice.

After the thorough and high-quality preparatory work that preceded it, it is all the more gratifying that the Consultation fulfilled all the expectations that we had for it, as a close reading of these proceedings will reveal. The cumulative effect of all the expert presentations was to formulate, in rational and convincing fashion, the main thrusts of various strategic options for furthering the implementation of patients' rights. The emphasis was on options that could be selected and adapted to fit the contexts of different countries, underlining the roles of different organizations, including international organizations. The response from the participants representing Member States is succinctly recorded in the positive conclusions and practical recommendations of the working groups that met during the

Consultation to consider the implications of the *Principles of the rights of patients in Europe* for future action.

I would like to thank the Government of the Netherlands, the Ministry of Welfare, Health and Cultural Affairs, and especially the staff of the Directorate-General of Health and the General and International Health Policy Department for their excellent cooperation and enthusiastic support to the Regional Office in the preparation and running of the Consultation. We have a particular debt of gratitude to Dr W. Cense of the Netherlands Red Cross, whose leadership in the chair contributed so much to the outcome of the meeting.

I would also like once again to acknowledge the contributions of the many technical experts who participated in the studies on patients' rights and to recognize the work of Professor Leenen, Ms Pinet, who was Regional Officer for Health Legislation at the time, and all the other members of the group responsible for the development of the guidance document.

Not least, I wish to express my thanks to all participants in the Consultation, both invited speakers and country representatives serving in the working groups, for their contributions to what was undoubtedly a significant occasion. The very real achievement of the Consultation, as reflected in its declaration, is that we now have a common European framework for action. The guidance document will be a solid reference source and a dynamic tool that will continue to generate new thinking in the health care system. Citizens and patients have the prospect of real partnership with providers and managers of health services in the process of care.

We have moved beyond the rhetoric of advocacy towards commitment. I pledge the continued cooperation and support of WHO to the efforts of all collaborating partners in countries and sister international bodies. Together we can and will ensure that patients' rights play a full part in our common mission to sustain the highest possible quality of care for all patients.

J.E. Asvall
WHO Regional Director for Europe

Part I

Setting the Agenda

1

Patients' Rights: Our Common Concern

A Welcome Address

H. d'Ancona

If you ask anyone what he or she believes is the most important thing in life, the chances are that the answer will be "good health". Research has shown that this is true of the Dutch, in any event. However, I doubt whether the Dutch are unique in this respect: nearly everyone in all the countries represented here would surely regard good health as one of the most important things in life. Being a patient is therefore something that affects us more deeply than anything else. Concern about health problems, coping with a body or mind that no longer functions as it should, dependence on others: all these have a profound impact on people's lives.

The rights of those who are ill and therefore vulnerable and dependent are thus a matter of great interest to all. I therefore welcome the initiative shown by the World Health Organization's Regional Office for Europe in bringing together representatives of the European Member States to discuss this very subject. It also gives me great pleasure to have this opportunity to open the proceedings here today.

Patients' rights are attracting more and more attention. By this I mean not only the more or less traditional concern of medical lawyers, but the growing interest that is discernible among the general public, patients'

WHO (eds.), Promotion of the Rights of Patients in Europe, 1-6.

organizations, health professionals and the authorities. World Health Organization studies have shown that this increased interest is a general trend, which can be observed in practically all the European Member States. I believe there are a number of reasons for this, reasons that are related both to changes in health care and to changes in the relationship between doctor and patient.

Concerning the changes in health care, I am referring here to increases in scale, in complexity and in the use of technology. While such developments should by no means be regarded in negative terms, they do entail certain risks, particularly when it comes to patients' rights. The increasingly business-like organization of health care could easily create a one-sided image of the patient, as a sufferer from a particular disease. Such an image tends to equate the treatment of the patient with the treatment of the disease, and to regard patients' rights primarily as the right to appropriate medical care.

But patients are, of course, far more than carriers of diseases. First and foremost, they are human beings and should unquestionably be treated by care workers with the respect that human beings deserve. In other words, patients' rights encompass more than the right to adequate treatment, important though that is. For example, patients also have the right to be well informed, to make choices for themselves, to express their own preferences and perhaps to refuse a proposed form of treatment. However self-evident such rights may appear, they can come under pressure from the developments in health care I have just outlined. And it is this awareness, I believe, that explains to some extent the growing interest in patients' rights.

The second reason I should like to mention is the fairly radical changes that have taken place in recent years in the doctor–patient relationship. In the past, partly due to the mythical status accorded to medical science, this relationship could be typified as one in which the patient had absolute faith in the doctor's authority. Consequently, patients did not ask or dare to ask too much, and preferred to leave decisions to the doctor. Trust was a quality that allowed patients to surrender themselves, as it were, to the doctor's care.

However, such absolute faith in the medical profession is more and more a thing of the past. I believe that this is because members of the public are becoming ever more articulate and because obedience to authority is less and less taken for granted in our society. Another reason is the popularization of medical knowledge. I cannot speak for other countries, of course, but I can vouch for the enormous popularity of the numerous programmes on health and medical matters that appear on Dutch television screens.

Today's patients want to be kept informed, to be able to see their medical records and to have a say in the treatment they are given. They also want their medical records to be kept confidential and their privacy to be respected. These are welcome developments, for they are indicative of a balanced, equal relationship between health professional and patient, a relationship in which each respects the other's rights and responsibilities, and they come to decisions together. It also means a relationship in which health professionals do not patronize patients, reduce them to a state of dependence or see every problem in medical terms. Rather, health professionals should encourage a sense of independence and self-reliance on the part of patients wherever possible. Research has shown that this is good medical practice, since well informed patients recover more quickly.

The increased interest in patients' rights is also apparent from this meeting, which has been organized by the World Health Organization and the Netherlands Government. I believe this to be a very important event. The document on which your deliberations are to focus over the next few days sets out patients' rights in a clear, orderly, balanced way. That document will therefore serve as a valuable guideline to the governments of the European Member States in the development of their policies on patients' rights.

However, the document is also of great importance to patients themselves and to health professionals. To the patients, it will be an instrument in their campaign for greater equality and, to the professionals, it will be of assistance in formulating professional ethics and codes of conduct.

This meeting will also boost the further formulation of patients' rights in other international fora. I refer here in particular to the Council of Europe, which has drafted a number of recommendations on this subject and is preparing a convention that will embody a significant number of patients' rights.

As you are here as the representatives of your various governments, I should like to say something at this juncture about the role governments can play in the matter of patients' rights. I shall illustrate my point with some play in the matter of patients' rights. I shall illustrate my point with some examples from the Netherlands – not, I hasten to add, to show how things *should* be done but to demonstrate what *can* be done. Needless to say, the interpretation of patients' rights may vary from one country to another.

Dutch Government policy accords high priority to improving the position of patients within the health care system. This involves giving patients greater choice, providing information, supporting patients' organizations, increasing patients' influence on the policies pursued by health care establishments and health insurance companies and creating sufficient complaint mechanisms. It also, most emphatically, means safeguarding the rights of patients.

The Government of the Netherlands has an important role to play when it comes to safeguarding patients' rights, because the Government is regarded as having a duty to protect the weak, and, as I said a moment ago, the patient is undoubtedly the weaker party in the doctor–patient relationship. Let me say, too, that there is widespread support throughout Dutch society for this protective role. Such support comes not only from Parliament and, naturally, patients' organizations, but also from the Royal Netherlands Society for the Advancement of Medicine, the organization that represents the medical profession. I am therefore particularly glad that the Society is making a significant contribution to this meeting.

Moreover, I believe that the support given to the Government and Parliament by health professionals themselves is of great importance. When we speak of the rights of patients, after all, we are also talking about the obligations of health professionals. And it is important that the professionals do not regard such obligations as a threat to or an encroachment upon their professional autonomy. It is essential for health professionals to regard respect for patients' rights as a vital element of the practice of their profession, for, however valuable statutory regulation may be, the real change in attitudes to patients' rights must, of course, take place in doctors' consulting rooms.

The principle underlying the statutory regulation of patients' rights in the Netherlands is that three conditions must be fulfilled. First, regulations must be easy for all those involved to understand. The rights and obligations of patients and health professionals must be set out clearly and concisely. Second, the regulations must be practicable. In other words, it must be possible to apply the statutory provisions in specific situations. Last, the regulations must naturally allow patients to enforce their rights if necessary.

In accordance with this principle, the Dutch Government decided to regulate patients' rights by means of a statutory regulation drafted for this specific purpose under civil law. The resulting bill is before Parliament as I speak. Indeed, the lower house has already given its assent. Once this measure enters into force, the general rights of patients will be embodied in a single instrument, and will no longer have to be derived from a fragmented corpus of statutory rules and case law, as is now the case. The decision to opt for a civil law instrument will make it possible for patients themselves to go to court if they believe that their rights have not been respected by a health care professional.

One question has recurred throughout the parliamentary debate on this bill to date. And I should like to conclude my remarks by putting this question before you, for it is one that, sooner or later, confronts every country considering regulating the rights of patients. The question is whether such regulation will damage the relationship between the health professional and the patient, which, after all, is one of mutual trust. And if patients can enforce their rights in law, will this not foster conflicts between patients and professionals?

I believe that it will not. I believe that a balanced statutory instrument, which recognizes both the rights of patients and the professional responsibilities of health professionals, will not damage the relationship of trust that exists between them. Conflicts do not stem from the statutory regulation of rights and obligations. On the contrary, they are a symptom of a relationship that has already been disrupted.

During the parliamentary debate, this relationship was compared now and then to marriage. Matrimony, too, is hedged about with many legal rules governing the rights and obligations of the spouses. But it cannot be said that these rules, as such, undermine the bond of trust between husband and wife or that they give rise to matrimonial conflicts. The aim of enshrining rights and obligations in legislation, whether they refer to the relationship between husband and wife or that between doctor and patient, is to prevent conflicts, or, should they arise none the less, to resolve them in a fair and equitable manner.

Ladies and gentlemen, my remarks on the policy of the Dutch Government and Parliament as regards patients' rights are intended merely as an example. As I said earlier, patients' rights may be interpreted in different ways in different countries, depending on such factors as culture, traditions of medical ethics and the nature of the legal system. Nor need you reach definitive decisions on this interpretation over the next few days. I believe that the main issue for this Consultation is for us to agree on the principles of the rights of patients in Europe, and that this whole matter is an important issue which should be high on the agenda of policy-makers in all the European Member States of the World Health Organization.

Let me conclude by saying that the Government of the Netherlands is honoured to welcome you to Amsterdam. May I wish you a productive and enjoyable meeting. Thank you.

2

The Rights of Patients in Europe: Progress and Prospects

J.E. Asvall

On behalf of the World Health Organization (WHO), I am very pleased to welcome all participants to this European Consultation on the Rights of Patients. The aim is to develop principles and strategies for the further promotion of the rights of patients within the context of health care system reforms, and to contribute to the enhanced understanding and acceptance of these rights.

With the support of the Government of the Netherlands, and in consultation with Member States, technical experts in the field have drafted a document entitled *Principles of the rights of patients in Europe* (see Chapter 4), which could be a meaningful and helpful tool for Member States in the development of their own policies. Although no formal adoption of this document is anticipated, it is the hope that it will be widely supported.

Patients' rights are a reflection of the importance of human rights, which have become increasingly recognized throughout the European Region in recent years. During the last two decades, and especially in the last few years, various social, economic, cultural, ethical and political considerations have given rise to a movement in Europe towards ensuring the rights of patients. The development of both the individual and social dimensions of patients' rights, taking into account living and working conditions and public health in its broadest sense, is very characteristic of our

WHO (eds.), Promotion of the Rights of Patients in Europe, 7-11.

times. This trend can be attributed to a return to the values inherent in fundamental human rights, such as notions of respect for the individual and for self-determination, on which the rights of patients are founded.

Today, well informed patients are beginning to assert these rights in their private dealings with professionals in the health field. Equally, developments in the systems of health care in many countries have implications for medical practice and the care of patients. Governments are paying increasing attention to such issues for many reasons, in particular the growing burden of bureaucracy (especially in hospitals); new developments in computer technology, data recording and management techniques; and the rapid advances in medical and health science and technology that have hastened the change in patients' expectations. There is a need to advocate new and more positive concepts of patients' rights, as in the Ottawa Charter for Health Promotion, which stressed the need for a reorientation of health services and new roles for health professionals as advocates.

Until the beginning of the 1970s, the health professional–patient relationship was defined primarily by the rules of medical ethics. During the last two decades, an approach to this relationship focusing more on legal provisions has emerged. With the introduction of the concepts of autonomy and self-determination, the relationship was gradually redefined in terms of a contract. The regulation of patients' rights underlines the importance and meaning of negotiation and patient participation. These are means to facilitate and improve the dialogue between the health care worker and the patient. This will, in time, significantly improve the quality of health care.

And such improvements are desperately needed. There are currently wide and haphazard variations in the quality of treatment and care throughout the Region. In order effectively to address the causes of these differences, clinicians, first and foremost, but also managers of health services, need information about where to intervene to improve quality. Quality of care is therefore fundamentally dependent on measurement. The time has come for a major commitment by health professionals and governments to develop and use such indicators to measure the outcomes of interventions in order to ensure more equitable and ethical care. Such systems must be suitable and they must be effective.

This is also related to the issue of the rights of patients to knowledge about the services they are receiving. While there are obvious difficulties in applying the concept of consumer guides to health care services, and these are issues that must be addressed very carefully, there is certainly scope for more development in the area of consumer information about the value and quality of health care services. It can only contribute to the strengthening of equity and ethical health care, if patients are as involved in the process as possible, through information and empowerment. It has been demonstrated that well informed patients make better partners in their care, and have quicker and more complete recoveries.

The central position of equity in health is a cornerstone of the WHO strategy for health for all, and is recognized by Member States as part of their pledge to the health for all movement. This stresses, *inter alia*, encouragement of individual choice and the opportunity to exercise it freely, and the commitment to build appropriate mechanisms to ensure the necessary quality of care. And, just as important in many respects, it will further the promotion of ethics in health care as recommended in the new target 38 on ethics and health, adopted in September 1991 by the forty-first session of the WHO Regional Committee for Europe in resolution EUR/RC41/R6. The target[1] states that:

> by the year 2000, all Member States should have mechanisms in place to strengthen ethical considerations in decisions relating to the health of individuals, groups and populations.

To assist and encourage progress towards the achievement of this target, equity and ethics will be the theme of the technical discussions at this year's forty-fourth session of the Regional Committee for Europe. It is becoming increasingly clear that equity and ethics are not merely of philosophical interest, peripheral to the health care debate; rather, they are central to making effective choices about policy needed to cope with the major health challenges faced today. If we neglect equity and ethics in health care, it will be disastrous for patients: leading to the exploitation of rich ones and the neglect of poor ones. Allowing unethical and unjust situations in health to develop is not only a problem for individual consciences but also has practical economic and social consequences.

The tremendous changes in the Region during the last years have reaffirmed the fundamental importance of the European policy and its

---

[1] *Health for all targets. The health policy for Europe*. Copenhagen, WHO Regional Office for Europe, 1993 (European Health for All Series, No. 4).

38 targets for health for all as a unifying framework for health development. The targets are a comprehensive health policy that provide a framework within which national adaptation and development on specific issues such as the rights of patients can take place in a coherent perspective and therefore contribute to balanced overall health development. Ethics and equity are vital considerations in this time when many health care reforms are being driven by a desire for cost containment.

The dramatically worsening economic conditions in the countries of central and eastern Europe (CCEE) and the newly independent states (NIS) of the former USSR are leading to intense pressure to cut spending on health care. This fact, coupled with poorer health profiles, increasing poverty and the unprecedented rise in unemployment, means that the most vulnerable groups in society are at ever greater risk, as the principle of free and comprehensive health care is increasingly placed in jeopardy. We must ensure that equity and patients' rights are not sacrificed to cost reduction. A two-tier system, allocating care on the basis of who can afford it, would not only be unethical, but would also undermine the foundations of the reforms that sought to improve the quality of life. We cannot support so-called reform in which the burdens fall more heavily on disadvantaged groups. This was reinforced most recently at the Vienna conference on the health of women in central and eastern Europe, where the particularly high burden borne by women was dramatically illustrated.

There is a debate throughout Europe about the nature and extent of the welfare state. Will the outcome be to increase the gaps between groups and between countries in access to care? Or will solutions be found that ensure equity as a fundamental principle? The way in which these challenges are met is a major test for the governments and health professions in Europe today. I believe that we have made a commitment, through the 38 targets of the European health policy, to ensure that equity, ethics and a respect for human rights will be central to our approaches.

In this connection, I believe that it is fitting that we are in the Netherlands, a country that has not shied away from a serious, open debate, even daring to face the issue of euthanasia in an open and courageous way. Many issues of care, such as care for an aging population, including terminal and palliative care, are of critical importance today. More countries will need to face these difficult and complex issues in the way our hosts have. Let us take the opportunity to learn from the presentations to this meeting on the Dutch experience.

I am confident that this meeting and the principles document will provide a common starting point for reflection, dialogue and decision-making in a wide range of professional bodies such as health authorities, health care providers, patients' organizations and even those with a wider social interest. It is work that can usefully support national action, as well as foster closer international cooperation in favour of the rights of patients in Europe.

The Regional Office for Europe has enthusiastically supported the whole process that has culminated in this Consultation. Through the study on trends in patients rights, the efforts of the expert group that formulated the principles document, and the numerous publications and activities of the health legislation programme, the work of the European Regional Office has formed a natural and synergistic complementarity with that of the Council of Europe. We recognize the important contribution of the Council in the critical area of health ethics, and are willing to work with it on the follow-up to the initiative we have taken here today to promote patients' rights. I look forward to our continuing discussion with our colleagues at the Council.

Finally, and most importantly, I would hope that throughout the Consultation we will be mindful that the development and promotion of patients' rights is one of the key ingredients to securing a better and healthier future for all Europeans!

Part II

Results of the Consultation

3

The Rights of Patients

Report on a WHO Consultation Amsterdam, 28–30 March 1994

Introduction

The European Consultation on the Rights of Patients was held by the WHO Regional Office for Europe and hosted by the Government of the Netherlands. The participants comprised some 60 people from 36 Member States of the WHO European Region. The participants represented a wide variety, not only of countries from all parts of the Region, with different processes of health care reform, but also of governmental, intergovernmental and non-governmental organizations. Thus, they could express the viewpoints and experiences of citizens, patients, health care providers, policy-makers and academics. The participants' task was to define principles and strategy to promote the rights of patients as the first step in a continuing initiative linked to the process of health care reform that was under way in most countries of the Region. Lists of the working papers and participants comprise Appendices 1 and 2, respectively.

The Consultation was the culmination of a long preparatory process. As early as 1986, the Regional Office carried out studies and surveys on the development of patients' rights throughout the Region, concluding with the

WHO (eds.), Promotion of the Rights of Patients in Europe, 13-28.

publication of *The rights of patients in Europe*[1] and the distribution of a draft document on the principles of the rights of patients. The strategy of the Consultation was to review patients' rights within the context of other emerging issues and trends, such as patient education, relationships between health personnel and patients, health education and social rights. The intention was to establish a broad rather than exclusively legal conception of patients' rights. This permitted the exploration of various possibilities for the adoption and observance of patients' rights in WHO Member States both in formal sessions and in informal discussion.

Discussion

The focal point of discussion was the document on the principles of the rights of patients, which had been prepared by an expert group convened by the Regional Office, and finalized after consultation with Member States. Short presentations focused on:

- the key issues in the document (information and consent, confidentiality and privacy, and rights to care and treatment);
- how the principles might be applied in practice and the resulting implications; and
- the wider political, social and ethical significance for health policy and for health care reform.

A special presentation on developments in the Netherlands showed how patients' rights could be promoted and the complementary views of physicians and patients/consumers. Then the participants formed three working groups. Their task was to identify the implications of the principles for policy, and the next steps to be taken in countries, depending on their invidividual circumstances, and by international organizations, to sustain momentum.

The groups' reports showed a notable consistency of the views expressed. There was general endorsement of the document *Principles of the rights of patients in Europe* (see Chapter 4). It offered essential guidance to be applied as appropriate by and within countries at various levels. It provided the basis for a continuing commitment to action. Its approach

[1] LEENEN, H. ET AL. *The rights of patients in Europe*. Deventer, Kluwer Law and Taxation Publishers, 1993.

could foster a spirit of partnership and mutual support among all parties concerned: governments and other public or other legally sanctioned bodies, patients' organizations and other nongovernmental organizations, members of the health and legal professions and relevant academic faculties.

In addition, the participants made a number of conclusions and recommendations. The principal recommendations were incorporated in a summary Declaration on the Promotion of Patients' Rights in Europe (see Chapter 4), which the participants adopted. The Declaration endorsed the principles of the rights of patients, commended the strategies for action identified below, welcomed closer cooperation between international bodies and proposed the monitoring of developments.

Conclusions and Recommendations

IMPORTANCE AND TIMELINESS OF PROMOTING PATIENTS' RIGHTS

1. Action taken now to promote patients' rights in the European Region would be a most timely contribution to the process of change in health care systems. Political, economic and social pressures were raising crucial choices in the organization, financing and management of the health sector, as well as fundamental issues of professional ethics and the need for new health legislative frameworks. Citizens' and patients' rights needed to be addressed within the context of these debates. For all countries of the Region, the primacy of patients' rights and health professionals' duties should not be lost under the pressure of economic and other forces.

2. As countries moved into closer relationships through their membership of international and integrational organizations, the need grew for a common spirit, a shared philosophy and culture of care throughout the Region. Nevertheless, differences between countries in the interpretation and realization of that common spirit would be respected, in accordance with their traditions and legal and other frameworks. Countries in political and economic transition had a special need for technical and other support, as they developed their own structures and strategies to promote patients' rights.

PRINCIPLES OF PATIENTS' RIGHTS

3. The participants took particular note of the WHO expert group's comprehensive understanding of health care: the full range of services for health promotion and protection, disease prevention, diagnosis, treatment, care and rehabilitation. This had particular significance for the concept of the patient and of patients' rights. According to the expert group, the patient encountered a wide variety of health care providers and fulfilled a range of roles, from sick and dependent person through client receiving advice to consumer or customer obtaining health products for his or her own use. This implied a continuum of health states, from a high level of wellness to permanent disability and terminal illness. The scope of patients' rights and, as appropriate, reciprocal responsibilities must therefore reflect this continuum.

4. Properly informed and educated patients, in partnership with their professional health care providers, were essential contributors to enhancing and maintaining the quality of the process and outcome of care. This partnership could only be truly effective, however, if it were matched by the development of mechanisms to give feedback to physicians and other care providers on the outcomes of their technical interventions, their efficiency in using resources and, not least, patients' perceptions of their behaviour in the care process.

5. Legal formulations of the rights and obligations of both providers and patients must have the clarification of roles and expectations as a primary objective. They should not be used to constrain the patient–provider relationship, or lead to defensive behaviour from either. They must always have an educational purpose, in addition to their use as a sanction in the event of the exceptional case of failure to fulfil a professional responsibility.

6. It was essential that provisions for patients' rights respond to the needs of everyone with a stake in health care. They must seek:

    - to promote and sustain beneficial relationships between patients and health care providers, and in particular to encourage more active patient participation;

- to reaffirm fundamental human rights in health care, and in particular to protect patients' dignity and integrity, and to promote respect for all patients, particularly the most vulnerable;
- to help patients obtain the fullest benefit from their use of the health care system, and, when necessary, to mitigate the effects of any problems they may experience with it; and
- to strengthen the opportunities for dialogue between patients' organizations, health care providers, health administrations and groups representing wider societal interests.

STRATEGIES FOR PATIENTS' RIGHTS

7. The development of a policy to promote patients' rights was the necessary first step; as soon as feasible, a carefully prepared strategy needed to be developed to ensure that the political intention was translated into a course of action that commanded the support of all parties involved. Such action would not follow automatically, but would take time to become fully effective. This meant that the people who were responsible for launching and guiding the action had to sustain their effort and sense of commitment.

8. While countries differed in legal frameworks, processes of health care reform, economic conditions and social, cultural and ethical values, certain common approaches could be adapted to the circumstances of each. The most positive consequence of the Consultation would be for all interested parties in each country to initiate or renew multiple strategies of implementation. These would probably need to include most or all of the following:

   (*a*) legislation or regulations specifying the rights, entitlements and responsibilities of patients and care providers (both health professionals and health care institutions);

   (*b*) professional codes, patients' charters and similar formal or quasi-formal statements of rights and obligations, to complement or supplement the relevant legislation or regulations (these should be drawn up in the light of understandings agreed between the representatives of citizens, patients, health care providers and policy-makers, and then periodically revised in response to changing circumstances);

(*c*) networking between and among patient and provider groups, recognizing the distinction between citizen and user participation;

(*d*) government support for the establishment and effective running of nongovernmental organizations involved in patients' rights;

(*e*) national colloquia and conferences to maintain the shared sense of understanding that has been reached between the representatives of citizens, patients, providers and policy-makers;

(*f*) sustained involvement of the mass media in informing the public, stimulating constructive debate and promoting awareness of the rights and responsibilities of patients, service users and their representative organizations;

(*g*) strengthening of training in communication skills at all levels of the professional education of providers, and introducing training in advocacy skills for patient and other user groups (both types of training implying the development of a proper understanding of the perspective and role of the other party); and

(*h*) commissioning of research of various types to help evaluate and document the effectiveness of legal and other provisions to support patients' rights, complemented by other research on health care providers' performance of technical tasks and aspects of patients' behaviour.

9. The pillars of any health policy that took proper note of the issue of patients' rights were equity and ethics in health and health action, as described in the WHO regional targets for health for all. Inefficient and ineffective practices in health care were unethical in themselves and perpetuated inequities by preventing the use of limited resources on people in need.

INTERNATIONAL ACTION

10. Support for patients' rights at the international level hinged on good cooperation between international organizations, such as WHO, the Council of Europe, the European Union, and relevant international nongovernmental organizations, such as the World Medical Association. Patients' rights needed to be the subject of continuing discussions between them and their members. Consistent policy positions,

coordinated strategies of implementation and an understanding of how their resources and competences could best be used were essential components of a sustained Region-wide movement to promote and protect the rights of patients and professional health care providers.

11. The forthcoming WHO Regional Conference on Health Policy would provide an important opportunity for increasing understanding of and disseminating strategies for the promotion of patients' rights in the European Region, and that the proposed WHO regional conference on health care systems in transition, to be held in Vienna in 1996, would address the rights, roles and responsibilities of both patients and providers. The Regional Office should monitor developments following from the Consultation and present the findings to the conference in Vienna.

Appendix 1

WORKING PAPERS

ICP/HLE 121/5	Principles of the rights of patients in Europe
ICP/HLE 121/6	Introduction to the study and the principles on patients' rights in Europe, by H.J.J. Leenen
ICP/HLE 121/7	Health professionals and the rights of patients, by M. Bonnel
ICP/HLE 121/8	Consumers' views on health care systems, by M. Calnan
ICP/HLE 121/9	Patient education and health education, by A. Deccache

Appendix 2

PARTICIPANTS

Albania

Dr K. Poro
President of the Order of Physicians, Hospital Centre of Tirana

Armenia

Dr H.R. Davtian
Department of International Affairs, Ministry of Health, Yerevan

Austria

Dr G. Aigner
Department of Public Health, Federal Ministry of Health, Sport and Consumer Protection, Vienna

Azerbaijan

Dr C.R.O. Ragimov
Head, Department of the Cabinet of the Minister of Health of the Republic of Azerbaijan, Baku

Belgium

Dr Lise Thiry
Conseiller au Ministère de la santé publique et de l'environnement, Brussels

Dr J.-P. Dercq
Inspecteur général, Ministère de la santé publique et de l'environnement, Brussels

Bosnia and Herzegovina

Dr Borisa Hrabac
Adviser to the Minister, Ministry of Health, Sarajevo

Bulgaria

Dr C. K. Nachev
Director, Department of Internal Medicine, Chief, Clinic of Cardiology, Medical Faculty, Sofia

Croatia

Ms Z.M. Matkovic
Senior Ministerial Adviser, Ministry of Health, Zagreb

Czech Republic

Dr P. Veselka
Ministry of Health of the Czech Republic, Prague

Estonia

Dr Ann Raadik
Therapist, Head of the Department of Internal Diseases, Keila Hospital

Finland

Ms P. Kokkonen
Director-General, National Boards of Medicolegal Affairs, Helsinki *(Vice-Chairperson)*

France

Dr G. Nicolas
Vice-président du Haut comité de la santé publique, Ministère des affaires sociales de la santé et de la ville, Paris

Ms S. Chaillet
Sous-direction des Systèmes de santé et de qualité des soins, Direction générale de la santé, Ministère des affaires sociales de la santé et de la ville, Paris

Germany

Dr K. Geyer
Counsellor for Legal and Social Affairs, German Embassy, The Hague, Netherlands

Ms Ellen Wolf
Leiterin der Unterabteilung Allgemeine Gesundheitsvorsorge, Berufe, Bundesministerium für Gesundheit, Bonn

Georgia

Dr Natalia Kazakhasvili
Head, Department of Economics, Ministry of Health of the Republic of Georgia, Tbilisi

Hungary

Dr P. Geher
Head of Division, Department of Health Policy, Ministry of Welfare of Hungary, Budapest

Dr Hana Páva
Legal Adviser, Legal Department, Ministry of Welfare of Hungary, Budapest

Iceland

Ms D. Palsdottir
Director of Legal and International Affairs, Ministry of Health and Social Security, Reykjavik

Ireland

Mr S. Benton
Principal, Secondary Care Division, Department of Health, Dublin

Israel

Ms Y. Kranoth
Senior Deputy Legal Adviser, Ministry of Health, Jerusalem

Italy

Dr G. Cimatti
Policy Secretary, Federative Democratic Movement, Rome

Kyrgyzstan

Dr A. Raimzhanov
Head, Department of Diseases of Internal Organs, Kyrgyzstan State Medical Institute No. 2, Bishkek

Lithuania

Ms T. Birmontiene
Consultant for Health Legislation, Department of Public Health, Ministry of Health, Vilnius

Malta

Dr A. Vassallo
Chief Government Medical Officer, Department of Health, Valletta

Netherlands

Ms A.-M. Alkemade
International Relations Officer, Directorate-General of Health, Ministry of Welfare, Health and Cultural Affairs, Rijswijk

Ms H. d'Ancona
Minister of Welfare, Health and Cultural Affairs, Rijswijk

Mr A.P.M. Bersee
Head, Section of Consumer Policy, Ministry of Welfare, Health and Cultural Affairs, Rijswijk

Dr W.H. Cense
Director General, Netherlands Red Cross *(Chairperson)*

Dr G. van Etten
Director, General and International Health Policy Department, Ministry of Welfare, Health and Cultural Affairs, Rijswijk

Dr B. Sangster
Director-General for Health, Ministry of Welfare, Health and Cultural Affairs, Rijswijk

Norway

Ms U. Nicolaysen
Senior Executive Officer, Ministry of Health and Social Affairs, Oslo

Dr Kari Sunderland
Deputy Director General, Norwegian Board of Health, Oslo

Poland

Dr J. Halik
Deputy Director, National Centre for Health System Management, Warsaw

Dr Jolanta Sabbat
WHO Liaison Officer, c/o Ministry of Health and Social Welfare, Warsaw

Portugal

Dr Joao Manuel Nunes Abreu
Director-General of Health, Lisbon

Republic of Moldova

Mr C.V. Pasecinic
Chief of Department of Health Services, Ministry of Health of the Republic of Moldova, Chisinev

Romania

Dr V. Belis
Director, Institute of Forensic Medicine, Bucharest

Russian Federation

Dr M.I. Verbitskiy
Deputy Director, Strategic Planning and Legislation Board, Ministry of Health of the Russian Federation, Moscow

Dr T.V. Gracheva
Chief, Division of Legislation, Ministry of Health of the Russian Federation, Moscow

Slovakia

Dr L. Šoltés
Head, Department of Medical Ethics, Postgraduate Medical Institute, Bratislava

Slovenia

Dr Polona Peternel
National Coordinator, "Patient-Friendly Hospitals" Programme, Clinical Centre Trnovo, Hospital of Internal Medicine, Ljubljana

Spain

Mr L.C. Martinez Aguado
Service of Attention to the Patient, National Health Institute, Madrid

Sweden

Dr Lena Jonsson
Head of Section, Department of Health Care, Ministry of Health and Social Affairs, Stockholm

Dr Lotta Westerhäll
Faculty of Law, University of Lund

The Former Yugoslav Republic of Macedonia

Dr J. Tofoski
Minister of Health, Ministry of Health, Skopje

Ms K. Burnazovska
Legal Adviser to the Minister of Health, Ministry of Health, Skopje

United Kingdom

Ms T. Funnell
Director, National Eczema Society, London

Ms N. Dennis
Head of Consumer Audit, College of Health, London

Uzbekizstan

Dr Y.D. Sakhybov
Director, Institute for Science and Research in Haematology and Blood Transfusion, Tashkent

Representatives of Other Organizations

Council of Europe

Mr H. Scicluna
Head of Health Division, Strasbourg, France

Hospital Committee of the European Community

Dr K. Schutyser
Leuven, Belgium

Dutch Patient and Consumer Organization

Dr A.F. Dekkers
Director, Utrecht, Netherlands

Royal Dutch Medical Association

Dr Joke M.G. Lanphen
Vice-President, Utrecht, Netherlands

European Forum of Medical Associations and WHO

Dr M. van Leeuwen
Executive Director, Health Council of the Netherlands, The Hague

International Organisation of Consumers Unions

Mr A. Chetley
London, United Kingdom

Temporary Advisers

Mr K. Barnard
Nordic School of Public Health, Gothenburg, Sweden *(Rapporteur)*

Dr M. Bonnel
Confédération des syndicats médicaux français, Paris, France

Dr M. Calnan
Professor, Centre for Health Services Studies, University of Kent, Canterbury, United Kingdom

Mr A. Deccache
Health Education Unit, Faculty of Medicine, Catholic University of Louvain, Brussels, Belgium

Dr S. Gevers
Professor of Health Law, Institute of Social Medicine, University of Amsterdam, Netherlands

Dr H.J.J. Leenen
Emeritus Professor in Social Medicine and Health Law, University of Amsterdam, Netherlands

Dr J.F. Martin
Médecin cantonal, Privat-docent et agrégé, Service de la santé publique, Lausanne, Switzerland

Dr R.G. Nypels
WHO Coordinator, Humanitarian Assistance Programme in Health, Skopje, The Former Yugoslav Republic of Macedonia

Dr A. Piga
Faculty of Medicine, University of Alcala de Henares, Madrid, Spain

Dr A. Prims
Professor, University of Leuven, Belgium

Dr Henriette Roscam-Abbing
Professor of Health Law, University of Utrecht, Netherlands

Mr B. Wijnberg
Deputy Director, Directorate General of Health, Ministry of Welfare, Health and Cultural Affairs, Rijswijk, Netherlands

World Health Organization

Regional Office for Europe

Ms K. Andersen
Programme Assistant, Training and Research in Public Health

Dr J.E. Asvall
WHO Regional Director for Europe

Dr J.A. Bury
Regional Adviser, Training and Research in Public Health

Mr G. Kirsch
Consultant, Training and Research in Public Health

Ms A. Rasmussen
Assistant, Director of Health Services

Dr C. Sakellarides
Director, Health Services

Dr M. Vienonen
Regional Adviser, Health Management

Headquarters

Ms G. Pinet
Senior Legal Adviser, Office of the Legal Counsel

Mr S.S. Fluss
Chief, Health Legislation

4

A Declaration on the Promotion of Patients' Rights in Europe

A WHO European Consultation on the Rights of Patients, meeting in Amsterdam from 28 to 30 March 1994, endorsed the document *Principles of the rights of patients in Europe* (see Appendix) as a set of principles for the promotion and implementation of patients' rights in WHO's European Member States.

The meeting gave detailed consideration to a wide range of possible strategies based on the principles presented in the document and on the recent and current experiences of participants. The essence of these strategies is presented below.

Strategies for the Promotion of Patients' Rights

The development of a strategy to promote patients' rights and responsibilities has to be carefully prepared, in order to ensure that the intention is translated into practical action which commands the support of all parties involved. Such action does not follow automatically, but takes time to become fully effective.

National situations vary in respect of legal frameworks, health care systems, economic conditions, and social, cultural and ethical values, but there are certain common approaches which can be appropriately adapted to the circumstances of each country. We encourage all interested parties in our

WHO (eds.), Promotion of the Rights of Patients in Europe, 29-44.

countries to initiate or renew multiple strategies of implementation, which will likely need most or all of the following components:

- legislation or regulations, specifying the rights, entitlements and responsibilities of patients, health professionals and health care institutions;

- medical and other professional codes, patients' charters and similar instruments, drawn up in the light of agreed common understandings between the representatives of citizens, patients, health professionals and policy-makers, and periodically revised in response to changing circumstances;

- networking between and among patient and health care provider groups, recognizing the distinction between citizen and user participation;

- government support for the establishment and effective running of non-governmental organizations (NGOs) in the field of patients' rights;

- national colloquia and conferences to bring the parties together to create and promote a shared sense of understanding;

- involvement of the media in informing the public, stimulating constructive debate and sustaining awareness of the rights and responsibilities of patients and users and their representative organs;

- better training in communication and advocacy skills for health professionals as well as for patient and other user groups, in order to further the development of a proper understanding of the perspective and role of all parties;

- promotion of research to evaluate and document the effectiveness of legal and other provisions and the various initiatives taken in the diverse contexts of the different countries.

International Action

Cooperation between WHO, the Council of Europe and the European Union in support of patients' rights would be further enhanced by action taken as a result of this Consultation. Consistency of policy positions, coordinated strategies of implementation and an understanding of how their respective resources and competences can best be used are essential components of a sustained European movement to promote and protect the rights of patients and their professional providers and advisers. International NGOs also have a critical role to play in promoting the rights of patients.

The forthcoming WHO Regional Conference on Health Policy (Copenhagen, 5–9 December 1994) will provide an important opportunity for further promoting patients' rights in Europe. The proposed WHO Regional Conference on Health Care Systems in Transition in Europe, to be held in Vienna on 25–28 March 1996, will also explore issues concerning the rights, roles and responsibilities of both patients and providers. We propose to WHO that the Regional Office should establish an appropriate mechanism to monitor developments in countries and to present the findings to the Vienna Conference.

Appendix

Principles of the Rights of Patients in Europe: A Common Framework

Introduction

1. Background

Social, economic, cultural, ethical and political developments have given rise to a movement in Europe towards the fuller elaboration and fulfilment of the rights of patients. New and more positive concepts of patients' rights have been advocated. In part, this has been a reflection of the central place given both to full implementation of the concept of respect for persons and to equity in health as a policy objective in Member States. As a consequence there is now greater emphasis on the encouragement of individual choice and the opportunity to exercise it freely, and the commitment to build mechanisms for ensuring quality of care.

Developments within health care systems such as their increasing complexity, the fact that medical practice has become more hazardous and in many cases more impersonal and dehumanized, often involving bureaucracy, and no less the progress made in medical and health science and technology have all placed new emphasis on the importance of recognizing the individual's right to self-determination and often on the need to reformulate guarantees of other rights of patients.

Simultaneously, the human rights movement has gathered importance in the world since 1945 when, in the Charter of the United Nations, Member States reaffirmed their faith in fundamental human rights. This was followed, on 10 December 1948, by the adoption of the Universal Declaration of Human Rights and, on 4 November 1950, by the signature of the

European Convention of Human Rights. Governments are more and more giving their active consideration to such issues. The World Health Organization's study of patients' rights in Europe shows that increasingly there are shared principles that are being adopted in a number of countries and which seem to be independent of the characteristics of a given country's health system. It seems timely to give this policy trend further momentum.

The present document is an attempt to formulate a set of patients' rights which reflects the evolving concepts and is relevant to the context in which health care will be provided in future.

These principles of the rights of patients in Europe have been drafted in full awareness of the work of others who have already been engaged in drawing up instruments specific to patients' rights. For the most part though, such earlier efforts were directed at particular groups or concerned with specific activities in health care or approached patients' rights from the perspective of the duties and responsibilities of health care providers and establishments. The present text is the result of an attempt to refocus these concerns from the patient's point of view as the user of and partner in health care in all its various forms. It has been deliberately couched in general terms, so far as possible avoiding reference to the circumstances of particular groups or illustrative examples. It is felt, however, that this exposition of general considerations embraces the basic principles and concepts to be adopted when promoting and guaranteeing patients' rights in a particular country or other situation. The text does not directly cover questions of implementation, since these are necessarily specific to a country or situation; it has nevertheless been drafted in the belief that these guidelines can be further elaborated within countries to suit their particular needs and circumstances.

Guiding Principles

In this text, the concept of health care is derived from the principles of the World Health Assembly resolution on health for all (HFA) (WHA30.43, 19 May 1977) and the related model of health care set out in the Declaration of Alma-Ata (12 September 1978). Health care thus embraces a full range of services covering health promotion and protection, disease prevention, diagnosis, treatment, care and rehabilitation. Accordingly, the patient encounters a wide variety of health care providers and fulfills a variety of roles, from sick and dependent person to client receiving advice to consumer or customer obtaining health products for self-administration. Furthermore, this variety of patient roles implies a continuum of health states from high-level wellness to permanent disability and terminal illness.

In the treatment of patients' rights, a distinction should be made between social and individual rights. Social rights in health care relate to the societal obligation undertaken or otherwise enforced by government and other public or private bodies to make reasonable provision of health care for the whole population. What is reasonable in terms of the volume and range of services available and the degree of sophistication of technology and specialization will be dependent on political, social, cultural and economic factors. Social rights also relate to equal access to health care for all those living in a country or other geopolitical area and the elimination of unjustified discriminatory barriers, whether financial, geographical, cultural or social and psychological.

Social rights are enjoyed collectively and are relative to the level of development of the particular society; they are also in some measure subject to political judgment regarding priorities for development in a society.

In contrast, individual rights in patient care are more readily expressed in absolute terms and when made operational can be made enforceable on behalf of an individual patient. These rights cover such areas as the integrity of the person, privacy and religious convictions. Although this text does address social rights, the main focus is on individual rights. The conceptual foundations for this treatment of patients' rights are for the most part laid on a number of intergovernmental declarations relating to human rights and freedoms. The intention is not to create new rights but to apply them in one coherent, comprehensive statement to the field of patients and health care. For similar reasons the text does not address general rights, obligations and liabilities, which are covered by the statutes and case law of each country.

A further issue arises concerning the place of exceptional limitations to particular rights of patients. For the most part these have been kept out of the text, in order to state the proposed rights as clearly and simply as possible. It is therefore pertinent to clarify here at the outset the nature of the principal forms of limitation. Exceptions to the rights of patients are usually anticipated in law. The guiding rule in such exceptions is always that patients can be subjected only to such limitations as are compatible with human rights instruments and in accordance with a procedure prescribed by law. In practice, this means limitations which apply for reasons of public order, public health and other persons' human rights.

In some situations, the reason for restricting the rights of the patient is an overriding interest of a third party (the so-called conflict of duties doctrine), i.e. the unfettered application of the patient's right would cause serious harm to a third party, there is no other means to avoid the harm and there is a reasonable expectation that the restriction would prevent the harm. In other situations a similar justification applies when the purpose is to avoid serious harm to the patient (the so-called therapeutic exception). As this document addresses general principles, these exceptional limitations to the rights of patients have mostly not been included.

Purpose of the Document

The principles of the rights of patients in Europe are offered as a contribution to support the growing interest in many Member States in the issues of patients' rights. In its scope and focus, this document seeks to reflect and express people's aspirations not only for improvements in their health care but also for fuller recognition of their rights as patients. In so doing, it keeps in mind the perspectives of health care providers as well as of patients. This implies the complementary nature of rights and responsibilities: patients have responsibilities both to themselves for their own self-care and to health care providers, and health care providers enjoy the same protection of their human rights as all other people. There is a basic assumption in the text that the articulation of patients' rights will in turn make people more conscious of their responsibilities when seeking and receiving or providing health care, and that this will ensure that patient/provider relationships are marked by mutual support and respect.

Patients should be aware of the practical contributions they can make to the optimal functioning of the health system. Their active participation in the diagnosis and treatment process is often desirable and sometimes indispensable. It is always important that they provide the relevant health professionals with all the information required for the purposes of diagnosis and treatment. The patient has an essential role, the reciprocal of the provider's, in ensuring that the dialogue between them is carried out in good faith.

Indeed, the role patients play in the appropriate delivery of health care should be underlined, especially in today's complex health systems which are largely supported by collective financial mechanisms and where the economic and equitable use of resources allocated to health care is an objective which can be shared by health professionals and patients alike. Equally, while patients' participation in clinical teaching must be subject to their informed consent, they should also be aware that the competence of future professionals in part depends on patients agreeing to be involved in their training.

Implementation

It is a matter for decision by countries how they might make use of a document such as this when reviewing their present policies on, practices in and legislative support to, patients' rights.

Although for the purposes of clarity of presentation some proposals are made in a clear- cut way, the text is a set of guidelines which could be used in policy discussions within countries and in the formulation or reformulation, as the case may be, of national policies, laws or official statements on any or all of the issues covered. However, it is hoped that this document will be of direct value to all parties, including patient and consumer bodies involved in health care, professional associations of physicians and of other health care providers, and associations of hospitals and other health care establishments.

2. Objectives

Against this background, the *Principles of the rights of patients in Europe* can be seen, in terms of content, as a document which seeks:

- to reaffirm fundamental human rights in health care, and in particular to protect the dignity and integrity of the person and to promote respect of the patient as a person;

- to offer for the consideration of Member States a set of common basic principles underlying the rights of patients, which might be used when framing or reviewing patient care policies;

- to help patients obtain the fullest benefit from their use of the services of the health care system, and mitigate the effects of any problems which they may experience with that system;

- to promote and sustain beneficial relationships between patients and health care providers, and in particular to encourage a more active form of patient participation;

- to strengthen existing and afford new opportunities for dialogue between patients' organizations, health care providers, health administrations and wider societal interests;

- to focus national, regional and international attention on evolving needs in patients' rights and to foster closer international cooperation in this field;

- to ensure the protection of fundamental human rights and to promote the humanization of assistance to all patients, including the most vulnerable such as children, psychiatric patients, the elderly or the severely ill.

3. Conceptual Foundations

In drafting these *Principles of the rights of patients in Europe*, the following intergovernmental instruments, which together offer a framework and a set of basic concepts which can be applied to the rights of patients, have been taken into account:

- the Universal Declaration of Human Rights (1948)
- the International Covenant on Civil and Political Rights (1966)
- the International Covenant on Economic, Social and Cultural Rights (1966)
- the European Convention for the Protection of Human Rights and Fundamental Freedoms (1950)
- the European Social Charter (1961).

The Rights of Patients

1. Human Rights and Values in Health Care

The instruments cited in the introduction should be understood as applying also specifically in the health care setting, and it should therefore be noted that the human values expressed in these instruments shall be reflected in the health care system. It should also be noted that where exceptional limitations are imposed on the rights of patients, these must be in accordance with human rights instruments and have a legal base in the law of the country. It may be further observed that the rights specified below carry a matching responsibility to act with due concern for the health of others and for their same rights.

1.1 Everyone has the right to respect of his or her person as a human being.

1.2 Everyone has the right to self-determination.

1.3 Everyone has the right to physical and mental integrity and to the security of his or her person.

1.4 Everyone has the right to respect for his or her privacy.

1.5 Everyone has the right to have his or her moral and cultural values and religious and philosophical convictions respected.

1.6 Everyone has the right to such protection of health as is afforded by appropriate measures for disease prevention and health care, and to the opportunity to pursue his or her own highest attainable level of health.

2. Information

2.1 Information about health services and how best to use them is to be made available to the public in order to benefit all those concerned.

2.2 Patients have the right to be fully informed about their health status, including the medical facts about their condition; about the proposed medical procedures, together with the potential risks and benefits of each procedure; about alternatives to the proposed procedures, including the effect of non-treatment; and about the diagnosis, prognosis and progress of treatment.

2.3 Information may only be withheld from patients exceptionally when there is good reason to believe that this information would without any expectation of obvious positive effects cause them serious harm.

2.4 Information must be communicated to the patient in a way appropriate to the latter's capacity for understanding, minimizing the use of unfamiliar technical terminology. If the patient does not speak the common language, some form of interpreting should be available.

2.5 Patients have the right not to be informed, at their explicit request.

2.6 Patients have the right to choose who, if any one, should be informed on their behalf.

2.7 Patients should have the possibility of obtaining a second opinion.

2.8 When admitted to a health care establishment, patients should be informed of the identity and professional status of the health care providers taking care of them and of any rules and routines which would bear on their stay and care.

2.9 Patients should be able to request and be given a written summary of their diagnosis, treatment and care on discharge from a health care establishment.

3. Consent

3.1 The informed consent of the patient is a prerequisite for any medical intervention.

3.2 A patient has the right to refuse or to halt a medical intervention. The implications of refusing or halting such an intervention must be carefully explained to the patient.

3.3 When a patient is unable to express his or her will and a medical intervention is urgently needed, the consent of the patient may be presumed, unless it is obvious from a previous declared expression of will that consent would be refused in the situation.

3.4 When the consent of a legal representative is required and the proposed intervention is urgently needed, that intervention may be made if it is not possible to obtain, in time, the representative's consent.

3.5 When the consent of a legal representative is required, patients (whether minor or adult) must nevertheless be involved in the decision-making process to the fullest extent which their capacity allows.

3.6 If a legal representative refuses to give consent and the physician or other provider is of the opinion that the intervention is in the interest of the patient, then the decision must be referred to a court or some form of arbitration.

3.7 In all other situations where the patient is unable to give informed consent and where there is no legal representative or representative designated by the patient for this purpose, appropriate measures should be taken to provide for a substitute decision making process, taking into account what is known and, to the greatest extent possible, what may be presumed about the wishes of the patient.

3.8 The consent of the patient is required for the preservation and use of all substances of the human body. Consent may be presumed when the substances are to be used in the current course of diagnosis, treatment and care of that patient.

3.9 The informed consent of the patient is needed for participation in clinical teaching.

3.10 The informed consent of the patient is a prerequisite for participation in scientific research. All protocols must be submitted to proper ethical review procedures. Such research should not be carried out on those who are unable to express their will, unless the consent of a legal representative has been obtained and the research would likely be in the interest of the patient.

As an exception to the requirement of involvement being in the interest of the patient, an incapacitated person may be involved in observational research which is not of direct benefit to his or her health provided that that person offers no objection, that the risk and/or burden is minimal, that the research is of significant value and that no alternative methods and other research subjects are available.

4. Confidentiality and Privacy

4.1 All information about a patient's health status, medical condition, diagnosis, prognosis and treatment and all other information of a personal kind must be kept confidential, even after death.

4.2 Confidential information can only be disclosed if the patient gives explicit consent or if the law expressly provides for this. Consent may be presumed where disclosure is to other health care providers involved in that patient's treatment.

4.3 All identifiable patient data must be protected. The protection of the data must be appropriate to the manner of their storage. Human substances from which identifiable data can be derived must be likewise protected.

4.4 Patients have the right of access to their medical files and technical records and to any other files and records pertaining to their diagnosis, treatment and care and to receive a copy of their own files and records or parts thereof. Such access excludes data concerning third parties.

4.5 Patients have the right to require the correction, completion, deletion, clarification and/or updating of personal and medical data concerning them which are inaccurate, incomplete, ambiguous or outdated, or which are not relevant to the purposes of diagnosis, treatment and care.

4.6 There can be no intrusion into a patient's private and family life unless and only if, in addition to the patient consenting to it, it can be justified as necessary to the patient's diagnosis, treatment and care.

4.7 Medical interventions may only be carried out when there is proper respect shown for the privacy of the individual. This means that a given intervention may be carried out only in the presence of those persons who are necessary for the intervention unless the patient consents or requests otherwise.

4.8 Patients admitted to health care establishments have the right to expect physical facilities which ensure privacy, particularly when health care providers are offering them personal care or carrying out examinations and treatment.

5. Care and Treatment

5.1 Everyone has the right to receive such health care as is appropriate to his or her health needs, including preventive care and activities aimed at health promotion. Services should be continuously available and accessible to all equitably, without discrimination and according to the financial, human and material resources which can be made available in a given society.

5.2 Patients have a collective right to some form of representation at each level of the health care system in matters pertaining to the planning and evaluation of services, including the range, quality and functioning of the care provided.

5.3 Patients have the right to a quality of care which is marked both by high technical standards and by a humane relationship between the patient and health care providers.

5.4 Patients have the right to continuity of care, including cooperation between all health care providers and/or establishments which may be involved in their diagnosis, treatment and care.

5.5 In circumstances where a choice must be made by providers between potential patients for a particular treatment which is in limited supply, all such patients are entitled to a fair selection procedure for that treatment. That choice must be based on medical criteria and made without discrimination.

5.6 Patients have the right to choose and change their own physician or other health care provider and health care establishment, provided that it is compatible with the functioning of the health care system.

5.7 Patients for whom there are no longer medical grounds for continued stay in a health care establishment are entitled to a full explanation before they can be transferred to another establishment or sent home. Transfer can only take place after another health care establishment has agreed to accept the patient. Where the patient is discharged to home and when his or her condition so requires, community and domiciliary services should be available.

5.8 Patients have the right to be treated with dignity in relation to their diagnosis, treatment and care, which should be rendered with respect for their culture and values.

5.9 Patients have the right to enjoy support from family, relatives and friends during the course of care and treatment and to receive spiritual support and guidance at all times.

5.10 Patients have the right to relief of their suffering according to the current state of knowledge.

5.11 Patients have the right to humane terminal care and to die in dignity.

6. Application

6.1 The exercise of the rights set forth in this document implies that appropriate means are established for this purpose.

6.2 The enjoyment of these rights shall be secured without discrimination.

6.3 In the exercise of these rights, patients shall be subjected only to such limitations as are compatible with human rights instruments and in accordance with a procedure prescribed by law.

6.4 If patients cannot avail themselves of the rights set forth in this document, these rights should be exercised by their legal representative or by a person designated by the patient for that purpose; where neither a legal representative nor a personal surrogate has been appointed, other measures for representation of those patients should be taken.

6.5 Patients must have access to such information and advice as will enable them to exercise the rights set forth in this document. Where patients feel that their rights have not been respected they should be enabled to lodge a complaint. In addition to recourse to the courts, there should be independent mechanisms at institutional and other levels to facilitate the processes of lodging, mediating and adjudicating complaints. These mechanisms would, inter alia, ensure that information relating to complaints procedures was available to patients and that an independent person was available and accessible to them for consultation regarding the most appropriate course of action to take. These mechanisms should further ensure that, where necessary, assistance and advocacy on behalf of the patient would be made available. Patients have the right to have their complaints examined and dealt with in a thorough, just, effective and prompt way and to be informed about their outcome.

7. Definitions

In these principles of the rights of patients in Europe, the following terms have been used with the meanings given:

PATIENT(S) User(s) of health care services, whether healthy or sick.

DISCRIMINATION Distinction between persons in similar cases on the basis of race, sex, religion, political opinions, national or social origin, associations with a national minority or personal antipathy.

HEALTH CARE Medical, nursing or allied services dispensed by health care providers and health care establishments.

HEALTH CARE PROVIDERS Physicians, nurses, dentists or other health professionals.

MEDICAL INTERVENTION Any examination, treatment or other act having preventive, diagnostic, therapeutic or rehabilitative aims and which is carried out by a physician or other health care provider.

HEALTH CARE ESTABLISHMENT Any health care facility such as a hospital, nursing home or establishment for disabled persons.

TERMINAL CARE Care given to a patient when it is no longer possible to improve the fatal prognosis of his or her illness/condition with available treatment methods; as well as care at the approach of death.

Part III

Background to the Principles of the Rights of Patients in Europe

5

The Study and the Principles of Patients' Rights in Europe

H.J.J. Leenen

Introduction

Health law and patients' rights, which form a part of health law, have been developing in Europe since the end of the 1960s. This is due to several factors. One is the evolution of medical science and technology, which intrude more and more deeply in the human body and mind and affect physical and mental integrity. Because their most intimate parts are touched upon by medicine, patients want to be secure that their rights are protected. In such a situation law has to play a role. Another reason for protection of the patient is his or her dependence on the health care system. In health care the individual easily is reduced to a case. His or her position is weak because of illness and the insecurity and fear it produces. A third factor in the development of patients' rights is the growing awareness of human rights in society, which is also reflected in health care. Human rights are at the centre of patients' rights.

The deeply intruding, sophisticated and bureaucratic health care system, on the one hand, and the dependent patient who often feels lost, on the other, have caused what I like to call a paradox of health care. The patient has to be defended against the health care system, which is only justified by the interest of the patient.

WHO (eds.), Promotion of the Rights of Patients in Europe, 45-56.

Governments have become more and more involved in health care, which in the past was mainly a matter for doctors. This is not only because the state has a duty to guarantee the rights of the citizens, but also because society wants equity in the distribution of scarce health care resources. The costs of health care place an increasing burden upon national resources and the equitable distribution of scarce health care facilities is a major issue. Social justice and the right to health care are at stake in ensuring this equitable distribution. Decisions as to this distribution directly affect the accessibility of health care. They embrace such issues as establishing a just insurance or other funding system for the costs of illness, planning health services, setting priorities, managing waiting lists and assuring quality of care.

The development of health law has brought national societies of health law and journals of health law to life in several countries, and universities have started research programmes and offered courses. Politicians, the public and the media have become interested. Not only nationally but also on the European level, health law is on the move. This month, the first issue of the *European journal of health law* was published. In the Council of Europe activities are undertaken in this field and conventions, recommendations and the like are adopted.

WHO Health Legislation Programme

On the European level a special role has been played by the WHO Regional Office for Europe. In 1977 the Regional Office started a programme on health law. In 1979, a health legislation unit was at work in Copenhagen. In 1981, an Advisory Committee on Health Legislation was established. Within this framework, experts in health law in Europe were brought together. Many activities were developed. European courses on health law were launched (the first one in Leuven in 1984), research projects were started and assistance to national governments was given. Ms G. Pinet, head of the unit, was the hub of this network.

Of the research projects, I must specifically mention a survey of teaching in health law,[1] a comparative study of trends in health legislation in Europe,[2] and a comparative study of the rights of patients in Europe.[3]

The trends study covered the approximate period 1970–1983. It was divided into five parts: health care consumers (patients), health care providers, health care establishments, the regulation of health care systems and financing. After the publication of the study in 1986, the Regional Office decided to undertake the more in-depth comparative study on patients' rights published in 1993. The rights were: informed consent, access to medical records, privacy and protection of data, secrecy and complaint procedures, with one chapter dealing with special categories of patients such as minors, incompetent adults, mental patients and subjects of research and experimentation.

This second study reports data collected in 1988 and 1989 and covering 27 countries of Europe. Since patients' rights were included in the earlier study, it was possible to study the further development of these rights in Europe between 1983 and 1988/1989. This resulted in a better insight into the trends in patients' rights in the Region.

Development of Patients' Rights between 1983 and 1988/1989

The study showed that, during the period covered, there was increased interest in patients' rights in the general public, organizations of patients and health professionals, consumer organizations, and legislators and other politicians. Universities and other academic institutions became more interested and a growing number of books, articles and other publications on patients' rights in Europe were published. Interest in ethical problems also increased. Ten main trends appeared.

1. Patients' rights, such as informed consent, confidentiality, access to records and the like, were further elaborated since the 1986 study. An

[1] AUBY, J. *Legislation sanitaire*. Paris, Masson, 1985.

[2] LEENEN, H. ET AL. *Trends in health legislation in Europe*. Paris, Masson, 1986.

[3] LEENEN, H. ET AL. *The rights of patients in Europe*. Deventer, Kluwer Law and Taxation Publishers, 1993.

example is the development of more specific norms regarding the contents of the information to be conveyed to the patient. A second example is that the rule of confidentiality has generated new rules on the protection of personal data in medical data banks or automated hospital information systems. Often in these new rules a two sided approach is chosen. On the one hand, individual rights are formulated and, on the other, obligations to safeguard security of data and confidentiality are imposed upon the custodians of the information system.

2. In the first study, a trend to reformulate doctors' duties towards patients' rights was found. This trend is exemplified by the rules relating to professional confidentiality. It is nowadays considered more a right of the patient than a duty of the doctor. In many laws and court decisions, confidentiality is formulated as a right of the patient. This trend appears to be continuing.

3. New rights have emerged since 1986. Particularly the right to privacy has given rise to new individual rights, such as the right to be informed when personal data are recorded in a data bank for the first time, and the right to have inexact or incorrect data corrected and to have data destroyed, as well as the rights to be informed about disclosure of data to third parties. Furthermore, it is recognized that protection of privacy relates not only to data, but also to the administration of medical procedures during the patients' stay in hospital or in other establishments. Also the right to a second opinion is becoming more and more accepted. Another new right is the right not to be informed if one wishes not to be. This right is, for instance, important when medical examination can result in knowledge about genetic predisposition.

4. With genetic testing, problems arise as to information before giving birth about genetic risks and the early prediction of a growing number of still latent diseases or health risks, which are likely to become manifest only years later. These diseases may be serious and medical science may not yet have answers in the form of treatment. Such information can have a deep influence upon one's life. Particularly in such cases, the right not to know provides an instrument to prevent receiving unwanted information. At the same time, such tests yield information that can be of considerable importance to relatives of the person being tested.

5. Still under discussion are the rights of the individual in relation to the use of one's cells or tissues for research. By applying new scientific techniques, bodily substances can increasingly yield information of a very personal nature. Such information has to be protected. The increasing value of the human body and parts of it for research and industrial purposes raises complicated questions about the legal status of human tissues and cells. The debate about these problems has not yet come to an end.

6. Also, new reproductive technologies have created new dilemmas. For instance, who has the right to decide on the use of gametes and of extra-corporal embryos and within what limits? Also, the right of the child to be informed about his or her origin and the legal position of the fetus *vis-à-vis* the rights of the pregnant mother, now that the fetus can be examined and treated within the womb, are under discussion.

7. At the other end of life, the right to die with dignity and termination of life upon request, when suffering has become unbearable, are issues that are under debate in many countries in Europe. In the Netherlands, the courts have accepted termination of life of a patient upon his or her request, but the legislation has not followed this trend. Only legislation for a reporting system was adopted.

8. Since existing formal legal procedures do not always provide an adequate answer to infringements of patients' rights, a trend exists to develop new procedures directed at handling patients' complaints. These procedures are rather informal and aim at solving a conflict more quickly than formal ones and, if possible, on the spot. Procedures chosen vary considerably between countries. General civil procedures are not always adequate and complaint procedures mostly do not provide financial remedy. Thus several countries in Europe are looking for arrangements to strengthen the position of the patient in civil law by addressing the problems of civil litigation. Examples are changing the burden of proof in favour of the patient and the introduction of no-fault compensation schemes.

9. In many countries, some categories of patients continue to receive special attention. This holds especially for minors and permanently or temporarily incompetent adults. There is a general recognition of the right to self-determination of these persons, although they may not be able to exercise it. More and more the law requires health professionals to respect the views of the incompetent patient. The formulation of criteria for

incompetence is important, the more so because the determination of incompetence is mostly left to the doctor. The study showed that, so far, no country in Europe has laid down such criteria in a law or a government regulation. The problem of incompetent adults will increase because, in many countries, not only the number of the elderly but also their life expectancy is increasing. Thus, provisions enabling persons to make decisions in advance about medical treatment to be given them in the event that they become incompetent are becoming urgent.

10. Finally, a rather new aspect in relation to patients' rights is the growing use, outside health care, of diagnostic and predictive methods that were developed for treatment purposes. This occurs during medical examinations that are required for getting a job or an insurance policy. There are two issues at stake. First, does a candidate for a job always have the duty to report existing information about his or her future health? Second, can a person be forced to undergo medical examinations that serve no health purpose, but that can produce data about, for instance, predisposition for a severe genetic disease for which no cure is available?

Individual and Social Rights

It will have been noted that the second WHO study dealt mainly with individual rights, but that the first included social rights. A distinction has to be drawn between individual and social rights. Individual rights, of which patients' rights are part, aim at the protection of the individual sphere and of individual liberty, whereas the goal of social rights, one of which is the right to health care, is to safeguard the paricipation of people in social goods. Social rights legally provide for an obligation of effort by the government, while individual rights are inherent to the individual as a human being. Individual rights are said to be of a negative nature because they ask government and society not to interfere with the sphere of the individual. Social rights are labelled as positive because they require government to ensure an equitable distribution of social goods and a just participation of the individuals in these goods. The right to health care aims at the quality and accessibility of health care: accessibility in financial as well as geographical terms.

From their nature, it follows that the content and scope of social rights are actually conditioned by the resources of the country. A social right is restricted to the available social goods. Thus, the right to health care, as a social right, does not justify a claim to provide methods of treatment or care that are not available. In contrast to social rights, individual rights, in principle, are not subject to conditions of scarcity. Although sometimes in daily language the right to health care is said to be a right of the patient, legally it is of a different nature. Formally speaking, the term patients' rights is better reserved for the individual rights of the patient.

Regulation of Patients' Rights

Regulation of patients' rights can take the form of legislation, professional codes and agreements and court decisions.

In the case of legislation, there exist several options. Patients' rights may be included in laws on specific subjects, such as organ transplants. They also can take the form of citizens' rights included in legislation that covers a specific topic, encompassing more sectors than health care. An example is legislation on the protection of privacy.

Another way of proceeding is to adopt a general law on patients' rights. Although development is rather slow, there is a growing interest in this type of legislation. As to the legislative technique of a general bill on patients' rights, two methods can be used. The first takes the horizontal relation between the patient and the health care provider as a basis and legislates patients' rights accordingly, as a contract between the patient and the health care provider within the framework of civil law, such as the civil code. This way has been chosen in the Netherlands. The other method stresses the role of the government in the protection of the patient. In that case, the use of administrative legislation is more appropriate. The administrative way was followed by Finland.

The difference between the two methods is less than might appear at first glance. The use of the administrative method does not prevent the patient whose rights are violated from starting a procedure according to civil law. The government preferring the civil option can also decide to give extra support to the rights of the patient by administrative ruling. So, for instance, legislation may enhance the position of the patient by administrative rules that impose obligations upon health care providers to respect patients' rights. Sometimes administrative legislation is even necessary, as, for instance, when the government elects to interfere with individual rights. An example is legislation on the compulsory confinement of dangerous psychiatric patients.

Professional codes can play only a limited role in the protection of patients' rights. They are adopted by groups of health care providers who represent only one of the parties involved in health care. The legal status of professional codes is weak. On the other hand, they are a useful instrument to create awareness among health care providers of their duties towards patients.

Agreements concluded between organizations of patients and health care providers are of a stronger legal nature. They represent a form of self-regulation. In the Netherlands, such a covenant was signed in 1990 between the organization of patients and the organizaion of doctors. Another was concluded with the organization of physiotherapists. But bi- or multilateral self-regulation in health care has its limits, especially when the parties to the covenant are unequal, when the stronger party may overrule the weaker one. For the government, this may and sometimes must constitute a reason to intervene. Such a reason may also be present when self-regulation does not meet the requirements necessary to be socially acceptable.

Although legislation and regulation are on the increase in Europe, the role of the courts in assessing patients' rights is very important. As long as legislation is deficient, the courts have to fill the gap. In many countries court decisions still are the major legal basis for the rights of the patient. Once legislation has been enacted, however, the courts will remain involved because of the need further to elaborate specific issues and to assess the development of new rights.

The Common Framework

Most significantly, the second WHO study showed that principles of patients' rights in Europe could be based upon common values and rules as to the rights of the individual citizen in health care. Despite many differences that exist in the Region, in essence all countries have adopted human rights and the wellbeing of the individual as the central issues in health. No matter the differences between countries in the formal legislation on patients' rights, the basic rules are similar.

One must also take into account developments in international political fora such as the Council of Europe and the European Community. A special role is played by the European Convention for the Protection of Human Rights and Fundamental Freedoms. The decisions of the European Commission and the Court of Justice of the European Communities have a strong influence on national law. There are many decisions that affect the health sector and patients' rights. The draft for a new convention of the Council of Europe on the protection of human rights and fundamental freedoms in the application of biology and medicine is expected to be published this year.

Building on the second WHO study, an initiative for elaborating a model declaration on the rights of patients was launched. The results of the study were to be the basis for drafting a text. This initiative, subsequently reformulated as the document *Principles of the rights of patients in Europe: a common framework,* was consciously connected to the health for all movement. The formulation of a set of such principles was seen as an important instrument for the implementation of many of the targets of the European health for all policy.

The text of the WHO document was developed by the working group of technical experts set up for this task. Although the study had provided us with knowledge about what was going on in Europe, we decided to stay in touch with the Member States, health care providers and patients during the drafting process in order to let the principles reflect opinions in Europe as fully as possible. A draft version was circulated to Member States and to national and international private organizations for comment. The comments we received were taken into account in preparing the final version that is the point of departure for this Consultation.

As to the status of these principles, the aim is to provide guidelines for the Member States. Since the implementation of rights is primarily a national matter, it was decided not to propose the document for formal adoption by the Member States. After this Consultation, however, it will serve as an important reference document for policy development on patients' rights on a national and European level, as for example in the Council of Europe and the European Community. It can also serve to promote awareness of patients' rights among health care providers and patients.

An introduction, which is designed to set up the elaboration of the principles, covers the background, the guiding principles and the purpose and objectives of the document. The principles themselves are couched in that form of international language that has somewhat of a legal nature, but the document is not a legal instrument. If the intention had been to prepare a document that was to be legally binding, it would probably have been of a less general nature and formally written exceptions to the rules would have been inserted. The general principles in the present text have to be adapted according to specific situations. Exceptions have only been included when considered to be useful for the understanding of the principle. An example is the therapeutic exception on the right to be informed in article 2.3.

As already mentioned, these principles of the rights of patients are based upon the results of the study on individual patients' rights. During the discussions of the working group it was decided to include a paragraph on the right to health care, which is a social right. Section 5 contains some guidelines related to care and treatment. This extension of the scope of the document was possible just because it is not a formal instrument but a set of principles. Formal legal aspects were no barrier against including both types of rights.

The principles are elaborated in six sections. In the first one, human rights and values are laid down. We have not invented them; they are internationally recognized and formulated in many declarations and conventions. The three following sections deal with classic patients' rights: information and consent, and confidentiality and privacy, and then there is the section about care and treatment. The final section deals with application, which is the field of national legal systems. Implementation of the principles requires careful attention: not only have the principles to be publicized, but ways and means have to be found to give them maximum effect.

There is indeed a need for a statement of principles of the rights of patients. National organizations of patients, doctors and hospitals, policy-makers, university staff and students repeatedly ask for a common European set of principles on the rights of patients. So the document will not only be useful to the WHO Member States of the Region; we hope it will also have a broader impact, even beyond Europe. Moreover, we have explicitly linked it with intergovernmental legal instruments of the United Nations and the Council of Europe. This underlines that it is not a separate initiative, but part of a broad national, regional and international movement. It makes explicit what is living in the minds and hearts of people.

Conclusion

In summary, patients' rights in Europe are on the move and, more and more, they are acquiring a legal base through legislation or regulation and through the courts. It is to be expected that new developments in science will result in further stress on the rights of the patient. The development of patients' rights occurs both at the national level, and internationally. As mentioned, the European Convention for the Protection of Human Rights and Fundamental Freedoms is already playing a significant role. In the Council of Europe patients' rights are increasingly a subject of conventions and resolutions. It is to be hoped that they will also be included in rules and mechanisms of the European Community. The principles document can usefully contribute to these developments.

Another incentive for the elaboration of patients' rights in Europe may result from cooperation between European health care systems. Such cooperation is necessary because diseases do not halt at national frontiers, because of the mobility of European citizens and because of the internationalization of science. The need for a more efficient use of scarce resources, especially in advanced medical care, may and should stimulate cooperation between national health care systems. Such cooperation will affect patients' rights in Europe. Because they have rights in one country, they will expect to have these rights in another country, as well. Again, the principles document can play a role.

Let me make a final observation. Sometimes patients' rights are seen as a source of tension between health care providers and patients. In my opinion and experience this need not be the case. Cooperation benefits both parties. Health care can function well only when health care providers and patients cooperate. A recent study concluded that 85% of the information required for diagnosis comes from the patient. Moreover, it appears from research that informed patients recover faster and stay in hospital for shorter periods. Recognizing patients as persons with rights and as partners is a prerequisite for their taking responsibility. As long as patients are treated as subjects incapable of making responsible decisions, patient education will not succeed. For the doctor, recognizing the patient as a partner is not only more satisfying, it is also professionally necessary. Quality of care depends on it.

The promotion of patients' rights is an important instrument in strengthening the role of the patient. Patient education and participation in medical treatment are others. Education and training are required for health care providers both in patients' rights and in communication with patients. Problems in communication stem not only from the patient, but also from the provider. One of our aims must be to find ways and means to make patients and health care providers aware that each gains by taking the other seriously.

6

The Issues

Information and Consent –
Henriette D.C. Roscam Abbing

In the document *Principles of the rights of the patients in Europe* (see Chapter 4), information and consent have been given a prominent place. With a view to their application in daily practice, some general background information and explanation are presented here for a clarification of the issues.

Though the concept of informed consent was raised early in the twentieth century, and was cited during the Nuremberg trials in 1947, the trend towards its legal recognition became apparent from the 1950s onwards. Its recognition has been stimulated because of concern with biomedical research, and is included in the World Medical Association's Declaration of Helsinki, 1965. The recognition of the right to privacy and to physical integrity in international human rights instruments of the United Nations and the Council of Europe has further stimulated recognition of the individual's right to self-determination in health care.

Recently, in the Netherlands, disciplinary action was taken against a doctor who knowingly withheld information from a patient on the

WHO (eds.), Promotion of the Rights of Patients in Europe, 57-63.

progressive nature of her disease until a few days before she died. Even then, the doctor did not inform the patient that death was imminent. The disciplinary court, in its consideration of this case, reaffirmed the principle of the right of the patient to clear information. This is considered necessary to enable the patient to take responsible decisions on treatment or stopping treatment, as well as on the settlement of personal and business matters. In another court decision in the Netherlands, withholding of information from a patient was considered as disrespect for the patient's interest, a mentality not worthy of a doctor. These two examples of Dutch court decisions on information and consent in health care can be supplemented by many others, including those from jurisprudence in other countries.

To be able to exercise autonomy, information and consent are fundamental requisites. Thus, paternalistic and protective attitudes in medical practice are by and large replaced by respect for patients' rights. The doctor–patient relationship has become, so to say, a two-way street. Decisions are taken in partnership on basis of informed consent by the patient.[1] The doctor is not confronted just with a disease, but with a patient. The informed consent requirement applies to day-to-day patient management in the diagnostic, therapeutic and care context. It applies to preventive medicine, to medical research with human beings and their medical data, to the use of organs and other bodily material for purposes other than the health of the person concerned, and the like. Below, the right to information and the consent issue are discussed in the usual diagnostic and therapeutic context.

Information and consent are the two most essential elements of the doctor–patient relationship. Information is a requisite to enable the patient to exercise self-determination. In case of emergency, the disclosure and consent requirements naturally cannot be lived up to if the patient is temporarily incapable of understanding. In that case, it is generally accepted practice that those medical interventions may be carried out that do not allow for postponement. The information and consent procedures apply as soon as the patient is again capable of understanding. Also, in the case of legally incompetent minors and mentally incompetent adults, the disclosure and consent requirements may be waived. However, there is a growing tendency to require the active involvement of the incompetent in the decision-making process as far as the incompetence allows. Also, in the case of an

---

[1] DYER, A.R. & BLOCH, S. Informed consent and the psychiatric patient. *Journal of medical ethics*, **13**(1), 12–16 (1987).

incompetent patient who has drawn up so-called advance directives when still competent, they need to be taken into account by the doctor.

Only very exceptionally may the doctor decide not to inform the competent patient. This may be the case if the doctor is convinced the information will have a significant adverse impact on and will cause serious harm to the patient. An example is the likelihood of suicide by the patient after communication of the medical prognosis. In that exceptional case, the doctor may appeal to force majeure and plead the therapeutical exception.

Though information and consent are closely linked, they do not coincide. The right to information encompasses more than information to obtain consent for a medical intervention. It pertains, for instance, to relevant facts after treatment: particularities of lifestyle to be followed and the like. Furthermore, from the perspective of the patient, the doctor has a duty to disclose to the patient any facts that are necessary to form the basis of responsible consent by the patient to the proposed medical intervention. Consent implies information and the free will and competence to decide.

Voluntary, informed consent is the legal justification for any medical intervention, whether therapeutic or non-therapeutic. Yet the right of the patient to information and proper consent procedures is a source of potential conflict between the judgement of the doctor, on the one hand, and the right to self-determination of the patient, on the other. There is a certain risk that the fact that medical science is not an exact science will be overlooked. There are always uncertainties, risks and unexpected findings. When confronted with the issue of informed consent, it should be realized that no person is exactly like another. The questions of how much the patient should be told, and by what standards the doctor's duty to provide information to the patient is judged, remain matters of personal judgement. They have to be decided upon in daily practice, on the basis of the physical and psychological condition of the individual patient.

Disclosure of information is a process with inherent limitations. Too many details may confuse the patient. Some medical interventions are self-evident in the frame of an overall medical procedure. For instance, pre-operative activities are in general supposed to be covered by the consent to the operation. This means that there is room for implied consent when the medical intervention is self-evident. Also, it is usually not necessary to obtain consent in written form. Mostly, a note in the patient's file that consent has been given is sufficient. The information to be provided to the patient should in any event be material, substantial and reasonable. A certain amount of discretion must be employed by the doctor, consistent with full disclosure of facts necessary to an informed consent.

A recent court decision in the Netherlands shows how delicate the matter of giving information with a view to obtaining consent can be. A medical doctor was found negligent by the court and ordered to make financial compensation because of the failure of a sterilization procedure. The woman in question was a strict Catholic, who declined abortion. Hence it was considered to be negligent of the doctor not to have informed her of the (even rather slight) risk of failure, because of the importance of that specific information to the woman in question. The doctor maintained that he had given this information, but he could not prove it, as it did not appear in the patient's file. It was his word against the patient's, the latter being accepted because the doctor could not prove otherwise. This case has caused rather some concern to the Dutch medical world. It was even suggested that courts would in future side with the patient and entirely reverse the burden of proof. There has been a rather defensive response to this court decision from the medical community.

This reactive attitude is also reflected in a forthcoming bill on the rights of the patient, which contains clauses on information and consent. In any event, in order to avoid liability, there is an increasing tendency towards the introduction of informed consent forms. It is evident that written information can be useful: for instance, leaflets with general information on particular diseases or procedures, and informed consent forms in the case of complicated medical interventions. Its effect is to inject a business-like approach into the doctor–patient relationship. Certainly it may be of value as a support to the process of communication of information. It can, however, never be a substitute for the information to be disclosed and the consent to be obtained in the individual doctor–patient relationship. Moreover, one should not overlook the fact that a signed consent form may be disregarded by the courts, unless it can be shown that the patient was given sufficient information in a way the patient could understand.

What does constitute sufficient information? Information to obtain consent for a medical intervention should include the type and nature of the intervention proposed, the reasons for which it is proposed, the possible complications, side effects and risks of the intervention, any alternatives, the expected benefits and the consequences if the medical intervention is not carried out. The most important element of the information is, of course, the prognosis. How far does the medical intervention provide an answer to the medical problem? Do the risks and complications of the suggested intervention exceed the expected benefits? To what extent should the likelihood of risks be communicated?

There is consensus that the "material risk" is standard. This implies that a risk is material when a reasonable person would be likely to attach significance to the risks in deciding to undergo or to forego a medical intervention. Disclosure of risk thus is measured by what a reasonable patient would want or need to know in the same or similar circumstances. Disclosure of risks that are reasonably foreseeable is generally required. Remote complications do not need to be disclosed, unless there is reason to believe that they might be of importance to the patient. An example is the duty to disclose the remote possibility of an allergic reaction to a highly allergic patient.

It follows from jurisprudence that, in the case of a patient who has consented to a medical intervention but has not been fully advised of the inherent risks, complications and possible side effects, the procedure has in practice been performed in the absence of real consent. There is then cause for an action on the basis of negligence, provided the patient can show that, if the information had been disclosed, consent to the medical intervention would not have been given.[2] In my view, it is a task for health care professionals, along with patients' organizations, to develop standards on what exactly a patient should know to be able to take decisions. Moreover, not only therapeutic interventions require information and consent, but also diagnostic interventions. It is important to realize that there is an increased overuse of diagnostic procedures, thus generating needless information.

There is always a factor of risk involved with diagnostic procedures and there are financial consequences. Yet in daily practice less attention is given to the need for information on and consent to diagnostic procedures. Though such consent sometimes may be implicit, explanation is still required. In a case where the doctor considers a diagnostic procedure as routine, it does not follow that the consent of the patient may be considered as being implied. Also, diagnostic interventions that are professionally considered as routine may constitute an infraction of a person's physical integrity.

---

[2] MORTON, W.J. The doctrine of information consent. *Medicine and the law*, **6**, 117–125 (1987).

They may, moreover, reveal information that could be serious or harmful to the patient. In particular, genetic information is very sensitive, because it also reveals information on biological relatives and it relates to one's off-spring.

It should also be noted that a right to information does not mean the patient is obliged to make use of that right. There is no obligation to be informed; information may not be given to the patient if he or she does not want to be informed. But there is no rule without exceptions. Thus, just as the right to be informed may be overruled by the therapeutic exception, the right not to be informed may be overruled exceptionally. There should, however, be a very serious reason to overrule the wishes of the patient, such as when not providing information is expected to cause serious harm to a third party. If the harm cannot be prevented in other ways, the doctor may then cite a conflict of duties.

Over the years, there have been many discussions on the right to information and the necessity of informed consent prior to any medical intervention. This necessity was not accepted by every medical doctor. It has, for instance, been argued that it would not be consistent with the trust the patient ought to have in the doctor, that the patient would not be able to understand the information, and that, because medicine is complex, the patient would not be in a position to exercise free judgement. Another argument that has been advanced is that information may frighten the patient into backing away from treatment. Also, it has been argued that disclosure of information is time consuming, and time is money. Furthermore, the informed consent requirement has been opposed on the grounds that it might stimulate litigation and reinforce defensive attitudes on the part of health care professionals.

Yet the fear that the patient will not understand the information is not justified. The doctor ought to develop skills to become understandable to and to communicate effectively with patients. Moreover, compliance with the rule of information and consent has more advantages than disadvantages. It does more than enable the patient to exercise the right to self-determination. Good communication has also been proven to contribute to patient compliance and to quicker recovery, possibly even shortening the stay in hospital, because the patient feels involved. It will save precious time because there will be less misunderstanding between doctor and patient and because it will avoid conflicts. If appropriate, adequate and understandable information is given, it will prevent rather than stimulate litigation.

The time it takes to inform the patient is easily compensated, because it creates and increases mutual trust and because decisions are properly thought over and knowingly taken. Information in health care will increase the patient's knowledge and thus stimulate the patient's own sense of responsibility. The therapeutic alliance will be strengthened if the autonomy of the patient is fully respected. Information and consent are fundamental safeguards of the rights of the patient.

Confidentiality and Privacy –

Paula Kokkonen

Introduction

Medical data and medical interventions belong to the most intimate sphere of the individual. The possibility arises that the disclosure of certain types of information collected in the course of medical examination may harm the patient by leading to various forms of discrimination and even to the violation of fundamental rights (according to the Council of Europe Recommendation R 81 (1) on Regulations for Automated Medical Data Banks). The conceptual foundations for patients' rights are for the most part built on a number of intergovernmental declarations relating to human rights and freedoms. These are listed in the document *Principles of the rights of patients in Europe* (section 3 of the Introduction). The intention in the document is not to create new rights, but to apply them in one coherent, comprehensive statement to the field of health and patient care. The guiding rule is that the patient can only be subjected to such limitations as are compatible with human rights instruments and in accordance with a procedure prescribed by law. Thus, limitations usually apply for reasons of public order, public health or another person's human rights. Limitations can also apply when there is a conflict of duties (recognizing the overriding interest of a third party) or the therapeutic exception can be cited (the need to avoid serious harm to the patient).

WHO (eds.), Promotion of the Rights of Patients in Europe, 63-67.

When drafting the document, we tried to keep in mind the interests of all patients and health care providers, and the complementary nature of rights and responsibilities. But we were also mindful of the most vulnerable people, such as children, psychiatric patients, the elderly, the severely ill, etc. and how best to promote their rights. In addition, the document is aimed at encouraging dialogue and interaction between all interested parties in health care. We are all travelling on the same train.

The Principles

Confidentiality and privacy are addressed in section 4 of the Principles document and my comments relate directly to the subsections of this paragraph. For convenience I first quote the subsections and then comment.

Subsection 4.1 states:

> All information about a patient's health status, medical condition, diagnosis, prognosis and treatment and all other information of a personal kind, must be kept confidential, even after death.

Confidentiality is seen as one of the most important prerequisites for a successful relationship between patients and health care personnel. Since Hippocrates, the matters listed in this subsection have been considered confidential. In a confidential relationship all kinds of information flow easily, and this information is often of very personal nature. There have been times when certain diseases have been labelled as the results of sin (today, at least in some people's eyes, it happens to be AIDS!). Such diseases have brought disgrace or shame on the person suffering from them. The reasons why information has to be kept confidential even after death are, *inter alia,* respect for the memory of the deceased and the protection of the privacy of the descendants or their families.

It is paradoxical that we simultaneously emphasize privacy and recognize through genetics, that we are not so independent of each other after all. We possess a lot of information about each other through our genes. In the Council of Europe Recommendation R 90 (13) on Prenatal Genetic Screening, Prenatal Genetic Diagnosis and Associated Genetic Counselling, the explanatory memorandum states that:

> genetic data is particularly sensitive and confidentiality must be assured. It is essential that its collection should be restricted and strictly controlled. Genetic data should only be collected and stored for purposes of medical care, diagnosis, prevention of disease and research.

Subsection 4.2 states:

> Confidential information can only be disclosed if the patient gives explicit consent or if the law expressly provides for this. Consent may be presumed where disclosure is to other health care providers involved in that patient's treatment.

Note that the law does not presuppose that the consent given by the patient should necessarily be written. "Explicit" leaves very little room for misunderstanding. To avoid unnecessary bureaucracy, consent can in obvious cases be presumed.

Subsection 4.3 states:

> All identifiable patient data must be protected. The protection of the data must be appropriate to the manner of their storage. Human substances from which identifiable data can be derived must be likewise protected

Confidentiality and privacy entail that all identifiable data must be protected. Data can be stored in documents, computer systems and also in human substances such as cells. There are, for instance, many recommendations from the Council of Europe concerning data protection, as well as a directive under preparation in the European Union.

Gene technology has brought about new powerful tools for identification and for producing information from human substances. This technology opens up an entirely new world: by analysing samples from one person, you necessarily get information about his or her relatives.

Subsection 4.4 states:

> Patients have the right of access to their medical files and technical records and any other files and records pertaining to their diagnosis, treatment and care and to receive a copy of their own files and records or parts thereof. Such access excludes data concerning third parties.

The very paternalistic view that long prevailed was that the patient's role was just to trust the doctor, who knows best; by increasing knowledge you increased suffering, and that was sufficient reason why patients did not have to know so much. But in the post-paternalist world of empowered and participating patients, responses to the questions of how much information is given to the patient, and whether the family members can be informed without the patient's consent, seem to vary from culture to culture in Europe.

Subsection 4.5 states:

> Patients have the right to require the correction, completion, deletion, clarification and/or updating of personal and medical data concerning them which are inaccurate, incomplete, ambiguous or outdated, or which are not relevant to the purposes of diagnosis, treatment and care.

There also seem to be different cultures even within one country in recording medical data. When searching to establish a diagnosis, you may, in difficult cases, have to record information related to various alternative diagnoses. Information stored for such specified and legitimate purposes must not be used in a way incompatible with those purposes; and the information has to be adequate, relevant and not excessive in relation to the purposes for which it has been collected, according to the Convention for the Protection of Individuals with regard to Automatic Processing of Personal Data.

It is not exceptional that, in the individual's medical record, you find criticism of the patient's outlook or habits, or indeed expressions of opinion that are clear insults. The following description is a graphic example taken from real life. A certain patient was described in his medical record as "an alcoholic who is drowning in his own flesh". The mere fact that patients have in general the right to know what is written about them in their medical files, probably keeps them "clean".

Subsection 4.6 states:

> There can be no intrusion into a patient's private and family life unless and only if, in addition to the patient consenting to it, it can be justified as necessary to the patient's diagnosis, treatment and care.

One should not moralize or impose one's own values, religion or convictions on patients.

Subsection 4.7 states:

> Medical interventions may only be carried out when there is proper respect shown for the privacy of the individual. This means that a given intervention may be carried out only in the presence of those persons who are necessary for the intervention unless the patient consents or requests otherwise.

The patient's consent is one of the most important prerequisites for having the patient participate in teaching. Getting the patient's consent is mostly a question of motivating the patient in an open and friendly way. Whether one succeeds may very much depend on the professional skills of the person asking for the consent.

Subsection 4.8 states:

> Patients admitted to health care establishments have the right to expect physical facilities which ensure privacy, particularly when health care providers are offering them personal care or carrying out examinations and treatment.

In privacy questions, we have made significant advances. Still, most hospitals have many patients, or at least more than one patient, in the same room. Patients' very intimate matters are often loudly discussed at the bedside, and all kinds of examinations are made in the presence of others. People who work daily in health care obviously often have difficulties in understanding how patients as individuals feel about different interventions and examinations, and that some people need more privacy than others. Applying the golden rule of ethics, "do to others as you would have them do to you", would probably save much suffering.

Care and Treatment –

André Prims

Previous presentations have addressed the issues of information and consent, and confidentiality and privacy. This addresses the rights of the patients in the field of care and treatment, which is a different category of rights, for the following reasons.

WHO (eds.), Promotion of the Rights of Patients in Europe, 67-72.

First, the rights on information, consent, confidentiality and privacy are individual rights. Those concerning care and treatment are social rights. Individual rights aim at the protection of the individual sphere and of liberty, whereas the goal of social rights is to safeguard the participation of people in the achievements of society. As to health, social rights are mainly expressed in the right to health care.[3]

Second, the first category of rights is mainly implemented through legislation, because these rights are based on general human rights. The second group of rights is mainly concerned with health policy and the organization and management of health care.

Third, the first group of rights is a part of civil law and of penal law and, in this respect, the courts are playing a very important role. The second group of rights is more a part of administrative law and the courts play a minor role.

Finally, the first group of rights can be considered as classical, whereas the second group of rights is relatively new. In the formulation of the second group, we have taken into account the targets for health for all adopted by the WHO Regional Committee for Europe. I would like to address the 11 rights that come under the heading of care and treatment in the principles document, and to give some explanation as necessary. In general I think that these rights are complete, clearly formulated and theoretically justified.

Subsection 5.1 states:

> Everyone has the right to receive such health care as is appropriate to his or her health needs, including preventive care and activities aimed at health promotion. Services should be continuously available and accessible to all, equitably, without discrimination and according to the financial, human and material resources which can be made available in a given society.

This subsection speaks about health care including preventive care and health promotion. For the first time, prevention and health promotion are mentioned in the list of the rights of the patients. Until now, the rights were limited to curative medicine. This is a very important development.

---

[3] LEENEN, H. ET AL. *The rights of patients in Europe*. Deventer, Kluwer Law and Taxation Publishers, 1993, p. 1.

Note the requirements that services for patients must fulfil. They must be continuously available, accessible to all and provided equitably and without discrimination according to the resources in a given country.

Subsection 5.2 states:

> Patients have a collective right to some form of representation at each level of the health care system in matters pertaining to the planning and evaluation of services, including the range, quality and functioning of the care provided.

Consumers' participation in policy-making for and the evaluation of health care is considered an essential condition of the success of the functioning of a health care system. Consequently, it is understandable that patients have a collective right to some form of representation in the health care system. The problems that could arise in the implementation of this right are:

- who is representing the patients
- how this representation can be organized
- how these representatives can be informed in an objective and efficient way about problems, needs and wishes.

Subsection 5.3 states:

> Patients have the right to a quality of care, which is marked both by high technical standards and by a humane relationship between the patient and health care providers.

Two weeks ago, the annual convention of the Belgian Society of Anaesthetists was held. The topic of the meeting was quality of care. Indeed, in theory, care means quality of care because poor care may not be given. Consequently, a right to care means a right to quality care.

The consumer is responsible for a demanding higher quality of services because, in the last analysis, it is the consumer's ignorance and indifference that allow poor-quality services to exist. The public has to be educated to distinguish between high and poor quality and to use the available services properly. It is commonly accepted that consumers' views on what constitutes high quality have been largely neglected. There are, however, an increasing awareness of the importance of these views among other groups, and growing pressure by consumers to make their views known and accepted. The problem, of course, is that the consumer's definition of good quality is perhaps the most nebulous of all.

So far, quality assurance programmes have almost exclusively been concerned with scientific technical quality, although there may be more need and also more possibilities for improvement on the side of the art of care, especially if one wants to take the qualitative expectations of the consumer into account. Several studies have amply demonstrated that, at least from the consumer's point of view, the behaviour of a health professional is an important qualitative aspect of care. The professional's human attitude towards the patient is fundamental in the patient's view of quality of care.[4]

Subsection 5.4 states:

> Patients have the right to continuity of care, including cooperation between all health care providers and/or establishments which may be involved in their diagnosis, treatment and care.

This right is clear and entirely justified, although there are many problems in practice. These are certainly observed in the field of continuity, but still more in the field of collaboration, which is currently one of the biggest problems in the health sector.

Who can bring about the cooperation needed between all health care providers and/or establishments? There are so many kinds of providers (specialists, general practitioners, nurses, pharmacists, physiotherapists, etc.) and establishments (hospitals, nursing homes, private practices, health centres, organizations for home care, etc.) that it is extremely difficult to achieve effective collaboration because of the different legislation, status, financing, etc.

Subsection 5.5 states:

> In circumstances where a choice must be made by providers between potential patients for a particular treatment which is in limited supply, all

---

[4] PRIMS, A. Quality of care: a patient's right? *In:* Dekker, E. & Van der Werff, A., ed. *Policies for health in European countries with pluralistic systems.* Houten, Bohn Stafleu Van Loghum, 1990, p. 175.

> such patients are entitled to a fair selection procedure for that treatment. That choice must be based on medical criteria and made without discrimination.

This right implies that:

- the public is informed about the fair selection procedure
- the public is informed about the medical criteria
- a system of control is built in
- the procedure and the criteria are regularly evaluated and eventually revised.[5]

Subsection 5.6 states:

> Patients have the right to choose and change their own physician or other health care provider and health care establishment, provided that it is compatible with the functioning of the health care system.

This is again a problem of organization and financing.

Subsection 5.7 states

> Patients for whom there are no longer medical grounds for continued stay in a health care establishment are entitled to a full explanation before they can be transferred to another establishment or sent home. Transfer can only take place after another health care establishment has agreed to accept the patient. Where there is a discharge home and when the patient's condition so requires, community and domiciliary services should be available.

I have one comment to make on this principle. Would it not be useful for the patient and for the authorities of the other establishments or services to have the full explanation confirmed by a written certificate?

Subsection 5.8 states:

> Patients have the right to be treated with dignity in relation to their diagnosis, treatment and care, which should be rendered with respect for their culture and values.

---

[5] *Kiezen en delen. Rapport van de Commissie Keuzen in de Zorg.* [Choosing and dividing. Report of the Commission on Choices in Care.] Ministry of Welfare, Health and Culture, 1991.

No comment is called for. This is a traditional and fundamental human right.

Subsection 5.9 states:

> Patients have the right to enjoy support from family, relatives and friends during the course of care and treatment and to receive spiritual support and guidance at all times.

In my opinion, the patient also has the right to refuse support and guidance.

Subsection 5.10 states:

> Patients have the right to relief of their suffering according to the current state of knowledge.

No comment is called for.

Subsection 5.11 states:

> Patients have the right to humane terminal care and to die in dignity.

This is a question of both ethics and the education of health care providers and organizations. Having regard for new developments in this field, the need to organize and finance palliative care inside and outside hospitals is probably indicated.

Part IV

Understanding the Challenges

7

The Context of Patients' Rights within the Health Care System

Jacques A. Bury

The purpose of these observations on the context of patients' rights is to stimulate a mapping of possibilities and to pave the way for envisaging strategic scenarios of desired changes.

It is necessary to distinguish between policy adoption, as a formal process, and policy implementation, as the practical outcome of an interplay between the main actors involved. Changes in societies and systems are not linear processes but the result of the influence of multiple factors and of complex interactions taking place within a specific context. The reality of patients' rights in a particular society at a particular time is indeed as much a determinant as a consequence of their formal expression in a policy or in legislation. It is a reflection of the relationships between the various groups of stakeholders involved.

Consider the full complexity of the interactions and their context. Pressures for change will come from the public and will be channelled, notably to their elected representatives: parliamentarians and governments. The role of mass media in influencing both the population and their representatives should not be underestimated. The context here will mainly be constructed out of the field of human rights and citizens' rights, then moving to rights of consumers of health services and finally patients' rights. However, pressure comes also from patients' associations, especially from

WHO (eds.), Promotion of the Rights of Patients in Europe, 73-76.

those representing sufferers from chronic diseases. Here the health care providers are their main target, and the evolving context of concerns is reversed, moving from patients' rights to human rights.

It is the goal of the pressures for changes that is the common point. That is why it has seemed useful to broaden the picture as much as possible, in order that the actors in the health field who want to promote changes can see more clearly how they can build upon the work of others, sharing commitments and opportunities to exercise influence. The differences to be observed between countries will be in the ways or approaches that policy implementation takes. These will be shaped by the national and, fundamentally, the cultural contexts. The differences will not be so much in trends, issues, or the observed involvement of particular actors, etc., but in the form and the strength of the actions that the actors take. In the attempt to understand these actions in their context, one has to take into account the relationship of patients with health care providers and of citizens with the health care system. This can be approached from three perspectives.

The Health Professional–Patient Relationship

This relationship is a cornerstone of ethics (the subject of European health for all target 38) and of codes of professional practice, and is central to the whole care process and outcome. It has been extensively studied from the perspective of the different human sciences, including psychology, sociology, anthropology, communication and law.

The principles in the WHO document *Principles of the rights of patients in Europe* (see Chapter 4) are obviously one of the main future means of shaping this relationship in theory and in practice. At the same time, the conditions of the practice and of the training of health professionals are important both as determining factors and as impact areas in the nature and quality of this relationship. It is also relevant to consider how both health professionals and patients will relate to another sort of emerging external influence: quality of care guidelines.

Consumers' Views on the Health Care System

The principles of the rights of patients are part of the global goal of social rights, which can ultimately be defined as safeguarding the participation of people in the achievements of society.

In terms of the health care system, besides the immediate individual rights of patients, these are mostly expressed as the right to health care, and, in particular, the importance of equity (the subject of European health for all target 1), which, along with ethics, is the cornerstone of the European policy for health for all.

These issues are of critical relevance to the current European debate surrounding health care reforms, and especially health care financing. There are strong grounds for expecting that the ethical debate over resource allocation will be the central question in the health sector by the end of the millennium. It seems very likely that the debate will then move to the whole issue of public funding and the role of the state, simply because health is, along with work, what matters most to people.

Patient Health Education and Public Health Education

Historically, the health education movement directed at the general public has been connected more with primary prevention and health promotion, while the development of patient education was associated with tertiary prevention and rehabilitation. Nevertheless, both have the same basic thrusts, ethics and principles, which culminate in the concept of empowerment.

Patient education seeks to empower patients to be active participants in their care, as opposed to being merely passive recipients of treatment administered by others. This includes educating patients about their diagnoses and the risks and benefits of various treatment options, as well as their rights to, and responsibilities for, their own health.

It strongly relates to their relationship with health care professionals. Historically, the key to this relationship has been the concept of compliance. It is the ambiguities, if not ambivalence, in the understanding and intended meaning of this concept of compliance that reflect the whole unfolding debate on the role of the patient and the significance of patient education.

On the other hand, health education is one component of the broader movement for health promotion. This movement encompasses both larger issues, such as the role of citizens in pressing for healthy or health promoting public policies, and the dissemination of education and information on individual behaviour and general lifestyles, as well as people's roles and rights as potential consumers or users of health services.

A review of the citizen participation literature concluded that there was virtually no reference to the relationship between citizen involvement and the development of individual participatory competence (C.H. Kieffer[1]). Hence the emphasis on this issue in this last approach to the rights of the patients.

Finally, it may be worthwhile to mention as a conclusion the title of a recent article that perhaps summarizes this evolution. In fact, it originated from the title of another article by Richard Smith)[2], the editor of the *British medical journal*, who commented on the unlimited expectations that both patients and health professionals share about the progress of medicine as a *folie à deux*, a sort of shared delusion. He spoke of the ethics of ignorance, which should remind us about the limits of the medical knowledge and indeed be a foundation block of doctor/patient relationship. Domenighetti[3] developed the thinking further in an article, whose title sounds like a challenging programme for the coming years: "From ethics of ignorance to consumers' empowerment".

---

[1] KIEFFER, C.H. Citizen empowerment: a developmental perspective. *In*: Rappaport, J., Swift, C. & Hess, R., ed., *Studies in empowerment: steps toward understanding and action*, New York, Haworth Press, 1984.

[2] SMITH, R. The ethics of ignorance. *Journal of medical ethics*, **18**: 117–118, 134 (1992).

[3] DOMENIGHETTI, G. *From ethics of ignorance to consumers' empowerment* (unpublished document).

8

Patient and Doctor Autonomy

H.J.J. Leenen

In the relationship between the patient and the health care professional two autonomies play a role: the autonomy of the patient and that of the health care professional. The position of the patient is based upon autonomy and self-determination, which are fundamental principles of society. Autonomy of the human being is not in the gift of the state. It is an inherent human right. This is not to say that human autonomy is unlimited. Each human right is exercised in a society of human beings and has its limits in the right of self-determination of other human beings. Autonomy is restricted by the principle that no harm may be afflicted on others. Also, common interest may entitle the state to impose restrictions upon the individual citizen. Yet there must be very strong arguments to justify encroachments upon individual rights and the principles of subsidiarity and proportionality have to be complied with. In most countries a law is required for such encroachments.

When citizens become patients, their legal position is not changed. An exception occurs when, because of mental illness that causes danger to others, a patient is legally detained. Patients normally have to be regarded as competent (that is, able to make their own decisions), despite the possibility that they may sometimes be emotionally affected by their illness. Even when people are ill, their autonomy is to be respected.

WHO (eds.), Promotion of the Rights of Patients in Europe, 77-78.

The doctor also has autonomy, not only as a person but also as a professional. In health law, the autonomy of the doctor is reflected in what we call the medical professional standard. This standard is derived from the state of medical science and experience and is worked out by the profession as an institution. The medical professional standard gives the doctor autonomy towards the patient in the sense that the patient is not entitled to ask the doctor to transgress that standard. The reply of the doctor to such requests has to be a firm no. He or she can even be liable if he or she carries out diagnostic procedures or treatment that are not in accordance with the medical professional standard. This implies that the standard, which gives the doctor autonomy towards the patient, at the same time limits his or her autonomy. In addition, rules of the hospital and other institutions, as well as social and legal rules, set limits to the freedom of the doctor.

So, in health care we have to deal with two autonomies that are both limited. The doctor has no right to treat the patient; the patient has no right to determine the kind of treatment in the medical sense. In normal circumstances, the patient decides whether he or she will be treated and, if alternatives exist, which alternative should be applied, but it is the doctor who determines what treatment and which alternatives exist. Within the relationship between the doctor and the patient, both autonomies must be exercised at the same time. This is only possible when patient and doctor cooperate. Both autonomies are strongly interconnected and an interplay between them is required. In other words, decision-making in health care is a common responsibility for the doctor and the patient.

In the Netherlands this idea increasingly is gaining ground, not only at the micro-level but also in the growing cooperation between organizations of doctors and of patients and between professional organizations of medical specialists and organizations of patients with a specific disease. In my opinion, the future functioning of health care will depend more on health care providers and patients becoming partners. Rights of patients have to be seen in this context. Doctors and patients both have to be educated for the role they have to play in health care. Ways towards a relationship of partnership between health care providers and patients need to be elaborated to ensure the implementation of the rights of the patient.

9

Health Professionals and the Rights of Patients

Marc Bonnel

This paper looks at patients' rights from the perspective of the doctor's relationship with the patient and with fellow practitioners and other health professionals. The evolution of the rights of patients has been reflected in new health legislation, but it also now needs to be reasserted that the rights of patients are fundamentally linked with the duties of health professionals. As Professor Villey recalled in the *Bulletin de l'Ordre médecins français* in October 1983, "doctors' duties *coincide* with patients' rights". One might further stress this link by noting that professional confidentiality or secrecy, regarded as a moral obligation for doctors, is indeed part of the patient's basic right to the protection of privacy, as reaffirmed in the Universal Declaration of Human Rights.

Professional Codes and Relationships and the Promotion of Patients' Rights

Professional codes of doctors and other health professionals (nurses, pharmacists, dentists, midwives, etc.) are a form of self-regulation developed by the profession concerned, without a say from patients or their representatives in the elaboration of the rules. They cannot replace formal regulations on the rights of patients, but they nevertheless play an especially

WHO (eds.), Promotion of the Rights of Patients in Europe, 79-85.

important role in guiding the conduct of those professionals and hence in ensuring that those rights are respected and enjoyed.

The doctor in particular is one of the key players in respecting and promoting the patient's rights. This is seen clearly in the frequent role of the doctor, especially in hospitals, as the coordinator of a medicosocial team of various professionals working with the physician (nurses, and midwives, dentists, physiotherapists, pharmacists, and others), transmitting to them information necessary for their tasks. A strong and trusting relationship among different health professionals that prevents misunderstandings is the basis for ensuring quality of care and other rights for patients. The doctor shares these new responsibilities with all other members of the medicosocial team, each member of which has a moral obligation. It is in this network of professional relationships that we see the significance of confidentiality, information giving, and access to medical records as three key areas in which patients' rights have implications for health professionals.

Health Professionals' Information-giving to Patients

Giving information to the patient is a duty. Health professionals must inform patients about their state of health, and make clear to them the risks of, and the effects to be expected from, the operation or other treatment proposed. The risks of poor communication between health professionals and patients include the potential for creating unrealistic expectations on the part of the patient, and thus possibly contributing to professional misconduct. Therefore, as far as possible, information for patients should leave no doubt or room for misinterpretation on their part, nor should questions be required to make the information more precise.

Giving information demands attitudes and skills that should be part of the training of health professionals. Being able to give information accurately and appropriately is not only the mark of the doctor's skill in communication, but also a prerequisite for consent.

In many countries, information is given orally by the health professional; in some countries, information giving has been explicitly dealt with in legislation. In Norway, the legislation states that doctors and other categories of health personnel shall give each patient information concerning health status and treatment. In the Netherlands the medical contract bill specifies that patients must be clearly informed by the health care professional attending them and the information must be given in writing if so requested by the patient.

In France, the Supreme Court of Appeal considers that the information should be adjusted in the light of the patient's capacity to understand. It can as a consequence be simple and approximate, but it must always be intelligible and honest. It is essential that all members of the health care team deliver consistent, appropriate and useful information tactfully, without disturbing the patient, having regard for his or her capacity for understanding, and minimizing the use of unfamiliar technical terminology. The differences between individuals and their cultures must be taken into account when considering the amount and manner of information given to patients. Information must be compatible with the patient's level of education, culture, mental health and intelligence, and if the patient does not speak a language in common with the health professional, interpretation must be available.

Confidentiality and Health Professionals

Today professional secrecy is primarily regarded and often described in legislation as the right of the patient to confidentiality. Secrecy is essential because the spread of information to a large number of persons beyond the health care team responsible for the patient could be detrimental to the patient's rights. The team is the front line for the necessary exchange of information, ensuring both that professional secrecy is preserved and that adequate answers are given to the patient's questions.

In some countries, secrecy is often formulated as a legal duty for health professionals. One of the reasons for doing so is to exempt them fully or partially from giving testimony in court proceedings. In Israel, the "evidence ordinance" provides that a doctor is not bound to give evidence on the treatment of an individual without the individual's consent. This privilege is extended to other health team members involved in the treatment, and to psychologists.

In the Netherlands, health care professionals are entitled to divulge information if maintaining secrecy would entail serious consequences for the patient, or for third parties, or is detrimental to the public interest. The decision is left to health care professionals to make after weighing the different interests involved.

Health Professionals and Access to Medical Records

Third parties might have an interest in personal medical data. Thus, the rights to privacy and confidentiality are interrelated. Accordingly in France, when a doctor gives up practice, or a patient changes doctors, the medical records are transferred to another doctor only with the patient's full agreement. In hospitals, medical records, which are held by medical secretaries (who are also responsible for maintaining secrecy), must be locked away in order to prevent unauthorized access. This could be particularly important, for instance, in the case of well known patients. It should also be noted that sometimes patients themselves try to put pressure on secretaries to release medical information to them that they are reluctant to request from the doctor.

Secrecy covers the relationship between the patient and the doctor or other health professionals, but the rules for this relationship are no longer sufficient for personal health data stored in data banks and administered by third parties. The data processed in automated systems may be liable to access by more people than would be individual medical files held under the direct supervision of a doctor.

In the Exeter experiment in the United Kingdom, the patient is given a health card with information put in by the family doctor. The patient thus maintains control of the medical information recorded by his or her general practitioner. On demand, the patient has the right to read all the information registered; only a diagnosis of AIDS or acute mental illness is not recorded. Normally, a patient's consent to communication of information to health personnel involved in his or her treatment is based mostly on presumption. In this case, however, it is actually the patient who becomes the instrument of communication. This health card is given by the patient to each health professional, who, through different access codes, may read whatever information may be necessary in order to give treatment.

Health Professionals and Formal Proceedings

Patients' rights are reinforced by penal, administrative or disciplinary legal proceedings. In some countries (France and Switzerland) the possibility of bringing a claim to a civil court depends on whether the doctor being sued works in a private hospital, since claims against personnel working in public institutions come under administrative law.

Often in a malpractice suit the patient must sue not only the health professional who was allegedly negligent in providing adequate care but also the hospital in which he or she is employed. In some countries, where health professionals employed in a national health service have the status of public officials or civil servants, civil actions may be brought against the state.

Administrative law may include standards on the availability, accessibility or quality of care provided by health professionals or institutions (as in Belgium, Denmark and Finland) or the rights of patients to be respected by health care providers (as in the Netherlands). In disciplinary law, specific arrangements often cover the disciplinary liability of particular health professions. In France, disciplinary review is left to the Conseil national de l'Ordre des médecins (National Council of Doctors), which delivers warning sanctions, fines and temporary or permanent suspension of the right to practise.

Should There Be a Law on the Professional–Patient Relationship?

For doctors and other health professionals, the initial contact with the individual, listening to the patient's needs, shapes the subsequent relationship between them, which evolves on the basis of mutual trust. It paves the way to establishing good diagnostic information and ensuring an efficient therapeutic follow-up. This is well understood and accepted by the patient.

In Latin countries, the strong individual relationship between doctor and patient has a sure foundation of reciprocal trust. The liberty of the patient to choose his or her doctor is balanced by the moral and codified obligation of the professional to provide care to the best of his or her knowledge and belief (*âme et conscience*).

In contrast, the Anglo-Saxon countries in particular, sharing a more explicitly collective approach to health, favour a legal framework that defines the rights and duties of patients, as well as those of health care professionals. The risk is that this framework becomes a strait-jacket that ends up standardizing the relationship, in which professionals respond to diagnoses purely in a technical manner, to the detriment of a more humane interaction between professional and patient.

On the other hand, in the countries of central and eastern Europe, the last 40 years or more have been characterized by a lack of any professional organizations with true independence from the state, as well as by laws that did not always function in accordance with the intentions stated in them. Consequently, in these countries, institution building for organizations of professionals and capacity strengthening in the legislative sector are clearly required. But this strategy must be pursued in such a way that avoids creating a constraining effect on the relationship between the health care professional and the patient.

Conclusion

A concluding fable or parable is perhaps timely as the most telling way of reminding ourselves of a basic truth. However important patients' rights and adherence to performance standards have become in the context of modern medical care, these can never be divorced from, still less replace, the inner ethical motivation of doctors or other providers to promote the health of their patients and ensure quality of care.

Once upon a time there was a centenarian, hitherto full of life, who suddenly felt a fever coming on one evening. He decided to call two doctors and he spoke to them frankly: "I am in pain. Feel my pulse, give me auscultations, examine my stomach. In fact examine me down to the last detail. Give me your opinion and then when I have heard you both I shall choose between you".

The first, Dr Quack, came forward and proposed X-rays, scanners and biological examinations. He then added, "Once I have this information I shall ask the medical team for their opinion, hand the results to my superior who will in turn calculate on a computer the cost-to-need ratio and quality-to-price ratio. The computer will then give us an answer and you will be cured".

The second, Hippocrates, pretending not to have heard anything, approached the old man and said, "My centenarian friend, I promise you, you will be treated in the way I myself would want to be treated".

The centenarian, in no hurry to die, put his trust in the second doctor's hands and joyfully lived on for another 100 years.

10

Citizens' Views on Health Care Systems

Michael Calnan

Background

The Declaration of Alma-Ata[1] states:

> The people have the right and duty to participate individually and collectively in the planning and implementation of their health care.

Two trends characterize today's health care scene in Europe: many countries are reforming their health care systems, and people are becoming increasingly interested in the services they receive and pay for, either as users or as taxpayers. The WHO Regional Office for Europe wants to bring these trends together by helping the reforms achieve their goals and by making people's views a criterion in the planning and quality of health care. Hence the Regional Office has, over the last two years, convened a working group on citizens' views on health care. Citizens' views are of particular importance in the context of this consultation, as patients' rights might be seen as one way that citizens' views are reflected and represented.

---

[1] *Primary health care.* Geneva, World Health Organization, 1978 ("Health for all" Series, No. 1).

WHO (eds.), Promotion of the Rights of Patients in Europe, 87-91.

The aim of this paper is to raise and discuss some of what a WHO working group thinks are the salient questions in this area.[2,3] More specifically, the paper examines some of the conceptual issues and considers how citizenship should be defined in the context of health care and why citizens' views should be heeded.

Citizenship – a Definition

Citizens, customers, clients, consumers, patients are all used in this context, sometimes to reflect subtle differences in approach, or sometimes interchangeably to represent those who need or use health care. However, to avoid this conceptual confusion, a distinction is made between citizens and users. The term consumer is inappropriate as, unlike consumers of other commodities, those seeking medical care are constrained by their lack of knowledge of the choices available and are dependent on professional expertise, especially in life-threatening situations. The intrinsically unequal nature of the relationship means that they are not in a position to shop around for the best buy and make informed choices, as those who advocate a business model of health care assume. Moreover, the distinction between the consumer and the producer of health care is not as clear as some might think, as ordinary people are also responsible for producing good health and preventing illness.

Citizenship means giving citizens what they need to allow them to contribute fully to society. Their needs include reasonable physical and mental health, which are to some extent shaped by broader social, economic, and environmental factors and cannot be adequately safeguarded by giving people rights as users of health care. While many citizens are users or potential users of the health care systems, citizens are defined not in terms of their use of services but by their status in the community. As citizens, we might have much wider concerns – not just about ourselves, but about our neighbours and other members of the community, both now and in the future. So, citizens' views encompass not just what individuals require for themselves and their families, but their broader concerns about what form of health care they want for a society as a whole. For example, citizens

---

[2] *Citizens' views on health care.* Report on a WHO meeting. Copenhagen, WHO Regional Office for Europe, 1992 (document EUR/ICP/PHC 214).

[3] *Citizens' views on health care.* Report on a WHO meeting. Copenhagen, WHO Regional Office for Europe, 1993 (document EUR/ICP/PHC 214B).

might be concerned with how they pay for their health care. Do they want a service free at the point of access for all citizens or do they want citizens to pay for their individual care? Do they want to pay for their health care through taxation, compulsory insurance and/or voluntary private insurance or direct payments or a combination of different methods of payment? They might also be concerned about the role of the state in the provision of health care, the extent to which it is the government's responsibility for providing health care and the extent to which government should intervene to protect the health of the community as a whole.

Users' rights, in contrast, are contextual and have little meaning outside the market place where caring takes place. Users' rights are only that small part of citizens' rights that relate to our experiences in the market place. For example, users might, within certain forms of health care system, be concerned about: the length of waiting lists, and waiting times for hospital care; the type of treatment they receive, particularly if they are suffering from serious illnesses such as breast cancer; whether they have access to medical care at night; whether their insurance will cover the full costs of their treatment for some major surgical procedures; or whether their family doctor has good communication skills and is someone they can talk to.

Why Should Citizens' Views Be Heeded?

One of the major reasons why citizens' views should be taken into account relates to the realm of political beliefs. That is to say, some have argued that taking the views and opinions of citizens into account, through increased participation in the policy-making or decision-making process, for example, may serve as a means of democratizing health services, thus making both the medical profession and the state more accountable. Alternatively, others have emphasized a somewhat different political philosophy concerned with issues of consumer sovereignty and the need for health care systems to be tailored to meet the demands and choices of its users. This tends to focus on individual demands, although, with the shift to explicit rationing from implicit rationing of health care in some countries, the public and community are increasingly being asked about their views on priorities for health care. In this way, purchasing authorities are attempting to be responsive to local views, although emphasis is placed on being responsive rather than on active community participation and representation in the policy-making process.

Why Should Users' Views Be Heeded?

There are at least four reasons that have been put forward to explain why users' views should be taken into consideration. First, there has been increasing emphasis placed on the quality of health care and there has been a growing recognition that a comprehensive assessment of health care should not only take into account clinical effectiveness, economic efficiency and equity but also include consumer opinions about health and health care. Thus, it has been argued that evaluation of health care should focus not only upon measures of clinical effectiveness and economic efficiency but also upon indicators of social acceptability of health care to the citizens. Thus, an essential component of a quality assurancc programme should be users' perceptions of the quality of health care.

Second, with the shift from acute to chronic forms of disease in the late twentieth century, coupled with changes in the age structure of the population, issues concerning the quality of long-term medical and social care come to the fore. With chronic forms of disease and disability, sufferers and their families play a more active part in management.

Third, citizens' views and levels of satisfaction may be important, not only as an outcome variable but also as a mediating variable that may influence, amongst other things, treatment compliance, which in turn might influence health status and medical outcomes. For example, there is evidence of a relationship between patient satisfaction with medical care and the rate of recuperation from illness and medical care.

The fourth reason relates to the realm of professional ethics and humanitarian concerns. The emphasis here is placed upon the altruistic concern of the doctor with the users' welfare. For example, some doctors emphasize the holistic nature of therapeutic care, which, by definition, requires that the concerns and interests of the user be taken into account. Also, in the context of ethics, some professionals emphasize the need to inform patients about the risks of different treatments or medical interventions and leave the decision up to the user as to whether they want the treatment or not.

Citizen-led Approaches

In each of the contexts discussed so far, the importance of taking into account the citizens' or users' views tended to be top-down, prescriptive policy in that the reasons for taking account of citizens' views were prescribed by governments, managers and/or health professionals. However, there is another context in which citizens' views have also been identified and that is where the initiatives extolling the views of the population or segments of it emerge from the community itself. Certainly, there are some initiatives, such as community development programmes or policies aimed at empowering the public, that receive resources from public authorities and aim to facilitate public participation. Others have emerged without direct support from above, such as self-help groups and voluntary groups who represent citizens or users who are unable to fully articulate their needs and preferences, such as those with learning or physical disabilities. This is the idea of citizen advocacy, where advocates pursue issues with relevant public authorities on behalf of their clients.

There are also initiatives related to citizens' and users' views that are claimed to have emerged out of social movements. The clearest example are those self-help groups in the area of childbirth and maternity care that aim to provide information for the health service user and to act as pressure groups for improving users' health. Some of these groups have actively challenged prevailing philosophies about childbirth on the grounds that they are not tailored to the needs and preferences of women.

Conclusion

This paper has attempted to clarify some of the conceptual confusion surrounding the term citizen and identify the range of contexts and reasons why citizens' and users' views need to be taken into account. The next stage of the group's work is to examine questions such as: how citizens' views are represented in health care systems in Europe, the mechanisms through which they are represented and the effectiveness of these channels and mechanisms for representing people's views?

11

Patient Education and Health Education

Alain Deccache

Interest in patients' rights first appeared in the 1960s, while health and patient education started right after the Second World War. Both are influenced by self-determination and respect for human values. The latter has obviously influenced the emergence of the rights of patients, which are an application and an adaptation of general human rights to the field of health, health care and medicine. Patients' rights have already been expressed and included in many charters and laws. There are therefore some basic questions that emerge, including the following:

- Why is it necessary to state and establish specific rights for patients; is it not possible just to use rights regarding all citizens that our countries and societies have already decided to acknowledge and respect?
- Is it for practical reasons (rights are theoretical) or because these rights are not respected in the health field?
- Is it possible to have patients' rights respected in health organizations, whether these are centres offering preventive services, general practitioners' offices or hospitals, and how can we enforce them?

WHO (eds.), Promotion of the Rights of Patients in Europe, 93-97.

A second set of questions then arises. These are concerned to establish and clarify the links between patient and health education and patients' rights.

- How do they interact and how can they mutually support each other?
- How can patient education, which is mainly a practice, meet patients' rights, which are mainly rules and theory?
- Can patient education help the implementation of patients' rights, and, if so, how?

If, as it should, patient education is to be considered as a means, a starting point, for the implementation of patients' rights, it also has clear limitations that must be acknowledged. A major problem is that it can be understood and applied in different ways, some of which are compatible with the rights of the patient, while others, such as traditional compliance-oriented education, create an opposite effect. Second, it only becomes operative when the care process is already in progress, when the person has become a patient within a health care organization. It cannot function as preparation of the citizen (child or adult) for the role of patient with its associated rights and duties. This preparation is a part of education for citizenship, a long-term task that should be the main concern of health education, directly linking disease prevention and the promotion of wellbeing to patients' rights and duties.

The Patients' Standpoint

For several decades, patient health education has been used in order to make patients more compliant to health recommendations and responsible for their own health. The dominant point of view was that of the health professionals and the focus was on patients' duties and responsibilities. With the shift towards a global and an educational model of health, the focus became the patients' needs and viewpoint. We have shifted from an expert approach to health to a more participatory and community-centred view, and from patient teaching to patient learning and education. Clearly, the focus on patients' rights comes from the same perspective. The search for ways to implement an active respect for patients' rights should be carried out using the experience of patient education. At the same time, it should be appreciated that those places where the practice of patient education is still in the process of being learned, are most unlikely to be the places where patients' rights are respected. The choice is between technocracy and democracy, remembering that only the latter leaves a place for both experts and patients.

Having the rights of patients respected requires that we define and have a clear understanding of the many concepts that are central to the formulation of patients' rights. The objective of meeting the patients' needs implies a prior decision, before it can be implemented, as to who defines those needs: experts or patients or both? The practice of withholding medical information from the patient, if his or her condition justifies it will remain unacceptable as long as the health professional is considered as the only one to decide on the patient's wellbeing. These two examples show that it will not be easy to resolve all the problems. But if we are able to accept the patient's viewpoint, then the patients' rights might be respected. It is a necessary rather than a sufficient condition.

Participation of Patients in Health Care

The patient health education movement has brought to our attention the concept of participation. The patient is no longer expected only to be compliant, but now also to participate, to provide the information about symptoms and health problems and history needed for a good diagnosis, and information about prior allergies, reactions and effects of treatments necessary for the choice of the appropriate therapy. Participation is of utmost importance for the success of the treatment, especially in chronic diseases and long-term prevention. Practitioners of patient education and health education have had to learn about participation. That experience and the fact that both compliance and participation can still be addressed together should help determine how patients' rights are to be respected.

Participation can only take place in a mutually balanced relationship, where the medical contract is clear and where patients and health professionals share rights and duties and freedom of will. If we are talking about patients' rights, we should not forget patients' duties and responsibilities, although for a long time they were the only part of the bargain. Professionals' rights and duties should also be listed and stated, as well.

Experience with patient education programmes has proven that the organizational aspects of care do influence the outcomes and results of education, and the resulting nature of the doctor–patient relationship. Some kinds of organizations and organizational structures are undoubtedly incompatible with education, participation and respect for human and patients' rights. Health care units with an autocratic structure and a hierarchy cannot be expected to facilitate respect for patients' rights, unless they are forced to do so.

Information for Patients

Informed consent is perhaps the most well known of all the issues directly linked to patients' rights that have long been important aspects of patient education and information. How patient education is able to bring about informed consent may be helpful in other matters of patients' rights.

To have patients' rights respected requires, first, that health professionals are ready to acknowledge those rights, and, second, that patients are well informed of their rights and duties, and the implications and consequences. Patient and health education have an important part to play in this information work. Although both were for a long time focused only on medical and health subjects, they are now more and more embracing psychological and psychosocial aspects of education. In other words, it is not only a matter of what to do but also how and why it is to be done. Education should help people to understand how they build their own representations of health and their behaviour. Their visions of the world and of life and health are directly involved, and so also should be their images and representations of their rights as patients and citizens. Non-health organizations, self-help groups and other organizations, have an important part to play here, alongside or in addition to health centres.

Quality of Care and Patient Education

Patient education is considered a major component in quality of care. In many cases and especially in chronic diseases, patients who do not (or are not helped to) comply with medical recommendations do not show any improvement in their health status. Patient education is an essential component of good quality of care, because it helps to solve the equation: correct diagnosis, plus adequate prescription, plus adherence to treatment (self-care).

So, if everyone has the right to the protection of health and to the opportunity to pursue his or her highest attainable level of health, then patient and health education is one of the means that should be used to reach this target and ensure that patients' rights are respected, because they do contribute to good quality of care and a better level of health.

Patient Education as a Bridge between Ethics and Rights

Patients' rights may be founded upon shared values, but in content they refer explicitly to the legal aspects of the relationship between the patient, the provider and the health care organization, such as a right to be informed, and to the rules that organize social interactions and life. Patient education is often more overtly or obviously concerned with values and ethics. The choices are not clear or easy to make; nevertheless, education necessarily involves a choice of objectives: teaching or learning, compliance or empowerment. In this perspective the role of patients' rights as laws can be properly and productively compared with professional codes as self-regulation, and bioethics as the expression of the meaning of care and the values of health professionals, to generate greater insight into the mutual stakes, needs and interests involved.

Part V

The Netherlands Experience

12

Patients' Rights in the Netherlands

A. Fons Dekkers

In this paper the focus is on the dynamics of patients' rights. Looking back at the evolution of patients' rights, we can define two stages. The first stage deals mainly with legal protection of the weak patient against the system and against the professional. The system is massive, bureaucratic, conceptually limited; the professional is powerful, and knows more about a limited area in which the patient happens to be weak. The professional has a financial interest, but also an interest in risk taking, or in taking the easy way. This first stage is still in evolution. In some countries it is just about to start; in other countries, such as the United States of America, it has a long story, going back to in the 1920s. The first stage in the Netherlands can be traced to the 1960s.

In the second stage of development, patients' rights serve as an instrument for stimulating equity and empowerment. They are an instrument to improve the system, to introduce more realistic dynamics into care and cure, to improve economic effectiveness, to improve quality assessment, and to have more open and relevant information available for decision-making. This is a different dynamic and a different ideology. It is important to make a distinction between the individual and the collective dimension here: it is on the individual patient's level and, at the same time, on the community level. As Calnan has pointed out, the main problem is the mechanism of representation, both of the individual patient, and as the

WHO (eds.), Promotion of the Rights of Patients in Europe, 99-105.

representation of a sort of collective awareness, which we could see as patients' awareness, users' awareness, or citizens' awareness.

In 1981 the Dutch government published a policy document, drawing attention to what governments or social organizations could do to improve the position of the patient within the health care system. This document was in fact addressing the issues somewhere halfway in between the first stage and the second stage of patients' rights. The document was an inventory of patients' rights as they were in the Netherlands in 1980. The conclusion was that patients' rights do not mean very much without a social context. Linkages to social interaction are needed. The first link is patient education, and the second is the participation and involvement of the citizen in the health care system.

To make patient involvement and participation possible, there needs to be an infrastructure of people, as both patients and citizens, who are organized around a theme, an ideology and a goal. It requires mobilizing different organizations, establishing a link between those organizations, and creating a body to direct this process. Regarding the Dutch situation in 1980, there were several hundred organizations around different diseases, and there were other related organizations, such as consumers' and political organizations. All of them were dealing with some aspect of health care, and all of them were stressing certain goals. But, in general, it was not an effective arrangement, because the effort was all too scattered, as it is in many other countries.

Since then, we in the Netherlands have been trying to combine all these different perspectives on health care and to create a federation in order to make it possible to coordinate all the different interests and to establish what they have in common. What does the average citizen and user of health care really have in mind? What is the type of quality expected? What is the type of need the user, the consumer, the citizen wants to have met by the system?

The Dutch National Federation of Patient and Consumer Organizations, on whose behalf I speak, is a coalition of all types of organizations, including consumers' organizations, patients' organizations, and organizations of elderly people. About 1.7 million people are organized within these bodies. We have 14 million people in the Netherlands, so 15–20% of the adult population is organized in some way around the themes in health care.

The Federation is trying to make visible in a general way the different aspects of being a patient, being a citizen, being a consumer, being a user. The Ministry of Welfare, Health and Cultural Affairs financially supports this effort in order to bring about a sort of equity and an equilibrium in society between professionals, third-party payers, consumers and other interests. Of course, there is a long way to go, but the concept is now well established.

It is important to stress that there are different concepts that are combined within the basic idea of this Federation. One important concept, indeed one important ideology, is that of personal independence, of self-determination. Patients' rights movements, at least in western Europe, have strong roots in the psychiatric setting. Fundamental rights are involved and have to be safeguarded in psychiatric institutions. Rather small organizations were very active in this field in the early 1970s in the Netherlands, the Federal Republic of Germany, France and the United Kingdom. Consisting of ex-patients, lawyers, politicians, philosophers, journalists, they were dealing with the concept of the self-determination of the human being. The message was essentially that a human being should not be made completely dependent on the limited concepts or belief systems of professionals who were in fact just dealing with one problem and not necessarily with whatever it was that a person was looking for and needing. They argued that people should be enabled to lead their own lives, to make their own choices, to decide their own values. The right of self-determination is, of course, the corner-stone of patients' rights, whatever the legal system that one deals with. We see the same emphasis on self-determination all over the world in organizations of disabled people. They are also dealing with the urge to live their own lives, not to have to depend on others, on professionals, just because they are disabled in some way.

This rather powerful ideology is one way of approaching patients' rights, and perhaps one third of the membership of the Dutch National Federation of Patient and Consumer Organizations comes from this particular tradition.

Another tradition is that of the organizations of inpatients of what are sociologically referred to as total institutions: nursing homes, psychiatric institutions and such. Here, other issues are at stake: certain democratic principles about being treated respectfully and being able to create one's own daily living environment. The key issue is mutual trust. The parents of mentally retarded children took a lead in this development, and people in psychiatric institutions were helped to establish their own councils or groups to support this idea. Some 5–10% of the membership of the Dutch Federation comes from this tradition of enabling people to defend their own interests by providing them with knowledge and skills to organize their own structures within the institutions.

There is another focus in the Federation, that of categorial patient interest groups. These relate to certain diseases such as rheumatic disorders, asthma, muscular dystrophy, diabetes. Such groups first flourished on a large scale in the United States and later in some European countries. The focus is on specific types of care and cure and the right to appropriate, high-quality treatment. This is not self-determination, but having one's needs taken seriously by the system. How do these organizations work for that goal? In the first place, they stress scientific research in different areas, especially in disease areas where there are small numbers of afflicted people. If only 100 or even 1000 people suffer from a certain disease in a country, there is not much available for them. The general practitioner does not know about it; the general hospital does not know what to do with it, and, because there is no money involved, there is no scientific interest. The people in these groups are trying to stress that, although small in numbers, they are important. Here we are dealing with diseases that last a lifetime, and therefore diseases that are really part of life. These people are trying to inform professionals within their specific fields about what their disease is all about. Here, we see education of professionals by patients, as well as education of patients by professionals, as a basic condition for the quality of care.

The second concern of these categorial groups is complementary care, the type of care that people can give each other. Patients, or ex-patients, who have come to terms with a certain problem are usually very well able to help others. They have knowledge from experience, and out of that experience they can help other people with the same problem. That is a type of experience a professional can never have, perhaps can never learn. It is very important that complementary care can be given by these people. It is very good for the health care system to organize this, to enable these people to be involved, to give them skills, to give them facilities for them to provide care, and to pay them for giving that care. They usually work on a voluntary basis, but it involves as much effort, as much trouble as for any professional. So one thing the Federation wants to stress is that this is a serious type of care: a serious complement to professional care.

A related field is the self-help movement. A self-help movement exists in most countries. It includes women's groups, grieving groups, coping groups and others. It is people saying:

> Give me some skills and I'll do it myself. I don't want to run after professionals. I want to do it myself. Not just because I want to be independent, or because I want to insist on my own self-determination. I simply think I can do it myself, so why should I depend on a professional?

This is a different ideology, and economical, besides!

There is yet another ideology, another movement: the consumer movement representing the general user who is not chronically ill. That is all of us, who from time to time take advantage of the medical system. What do we want from the system? This consumer movement stems from a broader movement of consumerism that comes from the United States. It started in the 1930s and became more visible in the 1950s. People such as Ralph Nader were trying to build a system around consumerism. It is about testing products, informing consumers, having the right to know and safeguarding people against the hazards from industry. It is about malpractice; legal affairs are very much involved in this ideology. But it is also about quality control.

What can be done when working on health care from the consumer's point of view? It means providing information on a large scale, enabling people to choose. This means having information available, not just from professionals, who have an interest in giving (or withholding) the information, but also on an objective basis. There are also organizations of elderly people and of women and of political parties or political parties' working groups, all dealing with the concept of the citizen within the health care system. So all this together makes a social movement of citizens and users in the health care system. Regarding the Dutch Federation, about two thirds of the total number of members who are dealing with the health care system come from this perspective and this tradition.

What are we in the Dutch National Federation of Patient and Consumer Organizations actually doing? First, and this is most important, we are trying to facilitate freedom of choice, which is the main patients' right in our opinion. Freedom of choice in fact anticipates informed consent, because, before one gets into the procedure of informed consent, one must be able to make one's own choice within the whole system and create relevant approaches with what the system offers. This involves making information available in general terms.

Second, the Federation works to define the real needs of patients from their point of view. The needs of patients are not the same as they are in the scope of the average professional. There are many surveys and research studies on this subject. When one looks into what a patient needs, and the quality a patient needs, it is generally agreed that 80% of what a patient needs is the same as the professional thinks the patient needs, but 20% is something different. These are needs coming out of a different context, having a different background. This 20% has to do with taking risks, with comfort or discomfort, with staying in an institution, with mobility, with being able to work, with being able to deal with things oneself. And it is this 20% of needs not covered by the system that makes people unhappy, that makes people dissatisfied with what they get. This state of affairs is not inevitable. Usually it is possible to help people get what they want, even the 20%.

Our third concern is to coordinate the strategies of interest groups, so we try to ensure that their effort and impact are not scattered, but focused on certain goals. And we try to be a symbol of solidarity: organizations of consumers and patients and disabled people working together for a good health care system. This is a symbol of solidarity within society: not every group for itself, but working for what they have in common. It is a very important concept, and a very important message to the world of politics.

Our fourth goal is to integrate citizens' and users' views within the system in many different ways. We try to build in the concept of quality from a patients' point of view within institutions, within the minds of professionals. Of course, this is a long-term goal, but one that has to be accomplished.

Last, we try to promote the implementation of patients' rights in general, that is, patients' rights as an instrument and as an ideology. In practical terms we have a large number of projects on these subjects. For example, we are working on a handbook on quality from the patient's perspective. I refer again to the 20% gap between what patients want and what the professionals do not offer. We are trying to produce a handbook, so professionals can read about the needs of patients. A second example is the network for filing complaints and providing information, assessing quality on the basis of people's perceptions of quality. We carry out surveys of patient satisfaction and try to make comparisons between institutions or between groups of professionals, noting their particular strengths. It is only the beginning of this development, but in, say, four or five years, it might be possible to point out the best hospital in the country. As a third example, we are trying to develop standard regulations jointly with professional bodies, such as the Royal Society for the Advancement of Medicine. We ran a conference on a model of patients' rights in the Netherlands. This was some years before the Bill of Patient Rights was embodied in the civil law. This was just an agreement between social partners, the physicians' organization and the consumers' organization, trying to address the basic concepts of patients' rights.

Let me, in conclusion, summarize and reiterate what I believe is the business of our organization. We have databases indexed on patients' needs. We provide books, leaflets, newsletters, all aimed at patient needs. We are trying to provide neutral information. We are organizing complementary care and counselling by experienced patients and ex-patients, and trying to support self-help groups in this whole area. We are dealing with aspects of legislation on and the planning of care from the users' point of view in general. Above all, we are working to create the conditions to make patients' rights and citizens' views really come alive within the Dutch health care system.

13

Involvement of the Royal Dutch Medical Association

Joke Lanphen

Introduction

The Board of the Royal Dutch Medical Association (RDMA) is honoured by the invitation to participate in this important European Consultation on the Rights of Patients. The RDMA has a long-standing tradition of activities in the field of patients' rights. We are glad to have the opportunity to share some of our experiences, observations and concerns with you. It is my sincere wish that these experiences and observations will contribute to the fulfilment of the aim of this meeting, which has been described as exploring strategies that may be useful in formulating national policies. In the first part of this presentation, I will try to clarify the viewpoint of the RDMA on the issue of patients' rights. In the second part, I will present an overview of the various ways in which the RDMA has been involved with issues in the field of patients' rights. Finally, I will make some concluding remarks on the document *Principles of the rights of patients in Europe* (see Chapter 4).

The Viewpoint of the RDMA

Until the beginning of the 1970s, the doctor–patient relationship was defined primarily by the rules of medical ethics. During the past two decades, a more law-oriented approach to this relationship has emerged: the

WHO (eds.), Promotion of the Rights of Patients in Europe, 107-113.

concepts of autonomy and self-determination were introduced. Gradually, the doctor–patient relationship, thus far characterized by the elements of mutual trust and confidence, was redefined in terms of a contract. A regulation of the doctor–patient relationship on the basis of standards, defined unilaterally by the medical profession, was no longer found acceptable. Due to a professional dominance of the doctor – which cannot always be avoided – an actual dependency and inequality may result for the patient. This could harm the trust that is so essential to the relationship between doctor and patient. A more formal regulation of the rights and duties of doctor and patient was seen as one of the means to compensate for the dependency of the patient and the inequality in the doctor–patient relationship. In the Netherlands, this development was influenced strongly by the enactment in 1983 of two new sections of the Constitution. Section 10 guarantees the right to privacy. Section 11 stipulates the inviolability of the human body. These sections came into force in 1988. They are of special importance for the field of health care.

With regard to this development, the RDMA has gradually adopted the viewpoint that a regulation of patients' rights can serve the needs of both patients and doctors. It would be far from realistic to suggest that this development is simply a matter of choosing between beneficence and autonomy. It is not a matter of either/or, but of both/and, and hence a matter of degree. When beneficence is overly dominant, an attempt must be made to achieve more autonomy. The patient will only benefit when these two elements are properly balanced. One should aim at an equilibrium between administering justice and doing good. All those concerned (doctors, patients, lawyers) should realize that the interaction between patient and doctor and their surroundings is often very complex and only to a small degree susceptible to influence by legal arguments.

This is not to say, however, that it is not worth while to develop a policy regarding patients' rights. Identifying and clarifying the fundamental rights of patients are necessary elements of any health care system. These fundamental rights create a basis on which the further development of the health care system in general and the patient–doctor relationship in particular can be built. A well balanced regulation on patients' rights underlines the importance and meaning of negotiation and patient participation. It recognizes both the importance of fundamental human rights and the therapeutic value of patient choice. Of course, a regulation on patients' rights should not be used in a dominating or rigid way. It must be seen as a means to facilitate and improve the dialogue between the patient and his or her therapist, thereby improving the quality of care. The activities of the RDMA in the field of patients' rights must be seen in this perspective.

Involvement of the RDMA

As a result of the position it has adopted on patients' rights, the RDMA has participated in activities and developments at both national and international levels. In the context of this meeting, it seems relevant to me to mention a number of these activities in order to illustrate the various ways in which national medical organizations may be helpful in the development and strengthening of patients' rights.

When we look at the issue from a historic perspective, one of the most important policy decisions made by the Dutch government was the creation, in 1978, of a committee on patients' rights within our National Health Care Board. The committee was headed by Professor Leenen, who was later instrumental in developing the WHO principles of the rights of patients that have been presented to this meeting. The Leenen committee included representatives of all important branches and organizations in the field of health care, including patients' organizations and the associations of doctors and hospitals. In the period between 1978 and 1982, the committee produced five reports on different aspects of patients' rights. These reports laid the foundation for a regulation of patients' rights at the level of an act of Parliament. The RDMA participated actively in the discussions of the Committee.

In 1987, the Dutch government published the first draft of a bill on patients' rights. The draft was clearly based on the reports of the Leenen committee. In May 1990, a slightly modified version of the bill was introduced in Parliament. In February of this year, only five weeks ago, the bill was accepted by the second chamber of our Parliament. The bill is now before the Senate. It is expected to enter into force in 1995. At various stages of the parliamentary debate, the RDMA has brought forward comments and amendments. These comments and amendments were aimed at creating a bill on patients' rights that could be characterized as a careful and balanced regulation, being neither vague nor rigid. During the last stage of the debate, in February of this year, some major sections of the bill were amended, partly as a result of comments made by the RDMA. In the opinion of the RDMA, the bill that is now before the Senate is a well balanced regulation, which must be seen as a useful and important contribution to our health care system.

Perhaps the RDMA's most important activity in this field has been the development, in collaboration with the National Patients'/Consumers' Platform, of a model doctor–patient regulation. The negotiations between the RDMA and the Platform started in 1984. They resulted in an agreement between the two organizations in 1990. The model regulation was widely accepted because it had the support of both the largest national medical association and the largest patients' organization. The agreement on the model regulation has in fact been a very important step in securing the acceptance of patients' rights among doctors and other therapists.

The model regulation must not be seen as an alternative to regulation at the level of an act of Parliament. The value of the model regulation is primarily that it bridges the gap between rules and regulations developed by the profession itself, on the one hand, and the rules and regulations drawn up by the government, on the other. The successful implementation of the future act on patients' rights requires a direct link between this act and the developments within the medical profession. The model regulation that was agreed upon in 1990 has proven to be a very useful tool in this respect. There is a strong resemblance between the contents of the model regulation and the contents of the bill on patients' rights. In the present situation it can be said that the model regulation anticipated the bill. The model regulation includes a number of topics that are not dealt with in the bill, such as referral to a colleague and the doctor's duties in case he or she decides to close down practice. With regard to some issues, the model regulation and the bill present different solutions. After the bill has been accepted by the Senate and the act on patients' rights comes into force, the model regulation will have to be revised and updated.

The activities of the RDMA at the international level have been aimed especially at the so-called Toronto Group. The Toronto Group is a network of 11 national medical associations, including those from Denmark, Finland, Iceland, Ireland, Norway, Sweden and the United Kingdom. The Toronto Group operates in the context of the World Medical Association. At the request of the Toronto Group, the RDMA has carried out a survey with regard to the patients' rights in the countries of the Toronto Group. The results of this survey were published in 1993. The report confirms the developments that have been described in the study on the rights of patients in Europe that was published in 1993 by Professor Leenen and his co-authors, under the auspices of the WHO Regional Office for Europe. In the countries of the Toronto Group, there is a clear trend to develop and strengthen patients' rights. In several countries, specific initiatives in the field of patients' rights have been developed. The report of the Toronto Group has been brought to the attention of the World Medical Association. The activities at this level and the present initiative of the WHO Regional Office for Europe may very well strengthen each other.

Finally, it is important to look at the level of the individual doctor. The responsibilities of the RDMA are not limited to influencing policy-makers at the national and international level. It is as important to ensure that the individual doctor in practice is properly informed and educated on the issue of patients' rights. It is the opinion of the RDMA that, as the national medical association, it should play an important role in the process of information and education. The RDMA has initiated a number of activities in this field, ranging from advising and assisting members who are faced with complaints or procedures regarding patients' rights to organizing meetings and seminars on this issue. The RDMA also favours proposals to increase the amount of time available for health care ethics and health law in medical training programmes.

In this outline of the involvement of the RDMA, the emphasis has been on the individual rights of patients. *Principles of the rights of patients in Europe* rightly mentions both the individual rights of patients and their social rights. The rights of patients obviously have two sides. Next to the need to protect human rights, there is the responsibility to ensure a just health care system, including the reasonable provision of health care. It is obvious that, although they stem from different legal backgrounds, the patient's individual rights, on the one hand, and his or her right to health care, on the other, should always be seen in connection with each other. The opinions of the RDMA on the social rights of patients are incorporated in our statements regarding the structure of the Dutch health care system. In the Netherlands, we are in the middle of an ongoing debate concerning the health care system. Issues related to the social rights of patients, such as equal access, volume of services and quality of care, are an important part of this debate. Both the RDMA and the Dutch patients' organizations have experienced the necessity to place the individual and social rights of patients in the context of the health care system as a whole.

Conclusions

The activities and viewpoints I have presented so far may suggest that implementing patients' rights in the Netherlands has never been a problem at all. Of course, reality was not that simple. It has taken us more than 15 years to reach the situation that we are in today. Over the years, certain developments in the field of patients' rights have met with severe criticism. In the beginning of the 1980s, the criticism was aimed especially at developments regarding the patient's right of access to his or her medical records. The RDMA still is reluctant with regard to the far-reaching right of access to records, which is laid down in the bill on patients' rights. Other concerns expressed by doctors were directed at the patient's right to information. It goes without saying that informed consent is crucial to any doctor–patient relationship. The concept of informed consent is the core element of patients' rights. However, the patient's right to information may be defined in a such a way that it turns out to be counter-productive, creating deception and legal procedures instead of fostering self-determination or a therapeutic alliance. This negative element may be triggered by developments in jurisprudence on medical liability.

In the Netherlands, we have recently witnessed some disturbing trends in this area, especially the increasing number of cases in which the court reversed the burden of proof to the doctor. From this point of view, the RDMA, along with medical associations from other countries, opposed the draft directive on liability of persons rendering services published by the European Community in 1991. In our opinion, the application of this directive to services provided in the field of health care would have resulted in a very unreasonable regulation of medical liability. Fortunately, it has been decided to exclude health care from this directive. These debates on specific issues will occur – and have occurred – in other countries. In our country, these debates are seen as necessary and, to a certain extent, unavoidable steps on the road to a just and well balanced system of patients' rights. They never provide any argument to leave the road. To do that would be to fail to address one of the most important issues in modern medicine.

Every now and then, debates on specific issues and problems will occur. What we should strive for is a context in which these issues can be debated successfully, without hindering or slowing down the realization of a patients' rights system in general. The activities of the RDMA, along with those of the Dutch government and of the patients' organizations in our country, have been aimed at creating such a context, both at the level of the legislation and at the level of the organizations of care providers and consumers. The contacts and activities at the latter level, and especially the model doctor–patient regulation that was agreed upon in 1990, have proven to be very helpful in the process of advancing and implementing patients' rights. It is not my intention to present the Dutch situation as a blueprint for other countries. That would be a rather arrogant thing to do. However, it is my belief that the Dutch experiences prove that it is possible to create an atmosphere in the field of health care, in which a regulation on patients' rights is generally seen as a very valuable addition to the doctor–patient relationship.

Moving from these experiences to the WHO *Principles of the rights of patients in Europe*, my conclusion is that this is an important document. The objectives mention the necessity to reaffirm fundamental rights, but they also include the promotion of beneficial relationships between patients and health care providers and the strengthening of opportunities for dialogue between patients' organizations, health care providers and wider societal interests. Its objectives and wording reflect a careful consideration of all relevant issues and interests. On behalf of the RDMA, I compliment the expert group that drafted the document on the result it has achieved. I sincerely hope that the document fulfils its purpose. The RDMA is convinced that the approach taken in the document will contribute significantly to the future quality of health care.

Part VI

Where Do We Go from Here?

14

Working Groups' Conclusions and Recommendations

A. Fons Dekkers

Following the presentations on the document *Principles of the rights of patients in Europe* (see Chapter 4) and related issues to be considered by the Consultation, three Working Groups were set up to review the implications of the document in their full context, to assess the prospects for their implementation in countries and to make practical recommendations for action.

Working Group 1 – *Moderators: Paula Kokkonen and Mikko Vienonen*

A Chinese proverb says that: communication is information and sympathy.

Prospects for Implementation in Countries

- Different situations need different approaches! In the war-torn countries of the European Region, concern with patients' rights could appear a luxury when all the essentials for life and care are missing.

- Even if a standard approach is not possible, it is important that a set of basic principles be made available to countries. This is the beginning of

WHO (eds.), Promotion of the Rights of Patients in Europe, 115-125.

a strategy. Sometimes the principles may have legislative consequences for a country, but often they will be used as guidance. The approach taken in a specific country to promote/safeguard patients' rights depends on the culture and legislative heritage. In some European cultures it is considered more appropriate to incorporate such principles in professional codes; in others, in binding rules, and, in yet others, in laws.

- In Europe we do not want to get into the situation where, as a rule, disputes are settled in the courts. If a country decides to promote patients' rights through legislation, the formulation of the legislation becomes very important. In Finland the law was the outcome of a long process (13 years), which can be traced back to the concerns of the professionals relating to confidentiality, informed consent and patient records. The law has considerably clarified the issues for all parties.

Education and Information for Promoting Patients' Rights

- The first right of the patient should be to know about patients' rights.

- It is a basic principle to defend the patient's right to autonomy and self-determination without forgetting the physician's right to autonomy.

- The promotion of patients' rights starts and ends with the education of health professionals. When we talk of the role of professional groups, we should not just mean physicians. Nurses, pharmacists and other groups of professional health care providers are equally important.

Cooperative Strategies for Promoting Patients' Rights

- The role of patients' organizations is crucial in the implementation of the principles of patients' rights. Associations representing sufferers from certain diseases may be more neutral in their approach than more aggressively minded consumer groups, but some countries have had good experiences of consumer movements.

- When patients' organizations advocate the rights of their particular group, they may, in doing so, step on the rights of others who lack strong and eloquent pressure groups. Special attention must be given to weak groups.

- There can also be confrontation between the authorities, professional groups and patient organizations. Experience has shown, however, that more information can relieve the confrontation.

- How to organize patient associations is a new and difficult challenge in countries in transition from centrally planned socioeconomic systems. Voluntary organizations by definition and by nature, should be voluntary, not led by professional groups or authorities. Even if (as is often the case) the initiative comes from certain enthusiastic physicians or nurses, the new associations must be encouraged and supported to operate independently.

- In western Europe many patients' organizations receive government support and have a long tradition of collaborating with the authorities. This creates a natural alliance for the promotion of patients' rights. But patients' organizations receiving substantial support from commercial interests, such as the pharmaceutical industry, may be vulnerable to manipulation.

- Possible partners in promoting patients' rights could be:
    - the mass media (television and the press).
    - unions of health professionals
    - church groups
    - schools
    - health insurance companies
    - parliamentarians and political parties.

The Right to Care

- Nobody has defined the content of good health care. An international organization such as WHO could make an effort to do so, but European countries are so different culturally, socially and economically, that meaningful international standards may not be feasible.

- In practically all countries, we know very little about the quality of health services. We should develop parameters through operational research and other means to assess the state of affairs in relation to patients' rights and quality of care.

- Budgetary constraints, cost containment and health care system reform inevitably bring up the issue of the basic basket of services in connection with patients' rights. Even though article 5.1 of the document *Principles of the rights of patients in Europe* says that services should be provided according to the resources available in a given society, it is difficult to set priorities and to draw the line on what is appropriate. We should not hide behind the budget, however; many things could be done that are not costly.

Future Role for WHO to Carry the Initiative Forward

- WHO should adopt innovative approaches to promote *Principles of the rights of patients in Europe,* such as organizing a consultation for medical journalists, preparing video presentations for international use, preparing an attractive book on the issue, etc.

- WHO should take up the issue in other WHO meetings. The health policy conference in December 1994 is a forum where patients' rights should be brought up as an important challenge. A second important event would be the 1996 conference on health care reforms.

- WHO should provide technical expertise to countries.

- WHO should develop case studies on patients' rights.

- WHO should cooperate with other international organizations. *Principles of the rights of patients in Europe* should be officially transmitted to the Council of Europe, which has been active in many ethical issues (such as organ transplant, confidentiality, bioethics, etc.). WHO and the Council of Europe should review together what both are doing. Duplication of the work should be avoided. A programme of joint and separate activities should be worked out and agreed. It would be important both to continue with present relevant initiatives, such as the WHO project on women's health, and to take up areas that are neglected such as migrants, socioeconomically deprived groups, etc.

- WHO should officially approach other European organizations such as the European Parliament, the Standing Committee of Doctors of the European Community, the Council for International Organizations of Medical Sciences, the European Public Health Alliance, etc. and Region-wide patient organizations.

Working Group 2 – *Moderators: Jean Martin and André Prims*

Prospects for Implementation in Countries

- Some countries have legal texts on patients' rights or are planning to have them. In other settings, declarations or charters have been promulgated, by public authorities or by private organizations or other international bodies.

- One should strive to get a formal text adopted and put in practice. As a first step, this can be done at the level of a hospital. It can be fruitfully linked with quality assurance efforts that are being implemented in several countries.

- One does not need a formally adopted charter or a legal text to make contact with the general public and/or partners, especially professional associations. It is possible and desirable, even in the absence of such documents, to assert or confirm that patients, although sick or wounded, are basically competent autonomous human beings, who have to be adequately and systematically informed and whose informed consent is systematically required save in exceptional circumstances.

Education and Information for Promoting Patients' Rights

- Patients' rights are part of citizens' rights. The public needs information that these rights exist. There is a place for advocacy and promotion by prestigious or otherwise well known personalities in the community. Information should be given as part of education in the appropriate use of health services and on a larger scale, of general education for citizenship.

- Issues related to patients' rights should be taken up in the education and training of all personnel, from those most highly trained to those with little or no formal training. In medical and other schools, this can be fruitfully done in a multidisciplinary fashion, with the participation of clinicians. It should take place in basic as well as in continuing education. One should not be afraid to adopt unconventional training methods, as well as newer communication and educational techniques and packages.

- Transparency and frankness without aggression are called for in discussions about patients' rights, even if it means accepting, and saying, that there are good and less good physicians, and that there are good and less good hospitals.

Cooperative Strategies for Promoting Patients' Rights

- It is very desirable, even necessary, to open a dialogue with the various institutional partners concerned, particularly professional associations of physicians, nurses and other health care professions, hospitals and health authorities, sickness funds, and consumer organizations.

- While adversarial/conflictual procedures might bring some gains, they are often short-term and limited in scope. The discussion and negotiation model is potentially more fruitful.

- In response to fears of medical associations and others that the principles of the rights of patients might stimulate complaints from the patients, develop bureaucracy and push physicians to practise defensive medicine, there is a powerful argument that well informed patients recover better and have shorter hospital stays.

- One practical possibility is to award certificates of good standing (or of quality or excellence) to professionals and institutions that prove to respect and promote patients' rights.

- As a relevant example from the health care arena, the baby-friendly hospital initiative was developed by private groups with the assistance of WHO and the United Nations Children's Fund (UNICEF), for the promotion of maternal and newborn care and especially breastfeeding.

A similar programme could be considered for patients' rights. Even though developments are called for at the national and international levels, successful actions can be launched locally and regionally.

- While good work can be done through voluntary efforts, one can hardly hope for rapid progress without investing resources. At the national and international levels, resources must be found for disseminating relevant information, for setting up appropriate mechanisms and for monitoring of and research into patients' rights.

Supervising the Application and Observance of Patients' Rights

- It is important that the person or body entrusted with this task be credible and appropriately neutral *vis à vis* the various groups concerned. The experience of various countries with ombudsmen or mediators has been quite positive.

- There might be a risk when the responsible person is paid by one of the partners (such as the hospital). But this risk can be overcome if the work done is of good quality and clearly serves the purpose of promoting the rights and wellbeing of the patient.

- Consumer or patient organizations can be successful in this role, if they consciously set out to prove their competence and build up a recognized legitimacy.

Future Role of WHO and Other International Bodies

- There is clearly a need for pursuing and strengthening the gathering, dissemination and exchange of information. Handy, attractive brochures and other publications are called for. WHO should continue its efforts in this field.

- The *Principles of the rights of patients in Europe* should be rapidly translated into all the working languages of WHO European Region, as well as into other national or regional languages.

- WHO must be proactive in the continuing promotion of patients' rights, including the organization of periodic meetings such as the present one. People working in this field need to be aware of what is being done in other contexts.

- The importance of acting in concert with other international bodies, particularly the Council of Europe and the European Union, must be stressed.

Working Group 3 – *Moderators: J. Gevers and A. Piga*

Prospects for Implementation in Countries

- The importance of the *Principles of the rights of patients in Europe* is as a common framework to be used and referred to at the national and sub-national levels. Such a framework can provide backing and support for development of policies and further activities concerning patients' rights within countries.

- In a number of countries, legislation or forms of self-regulation (such as codes of conduct) already cover at least part of the patients' rights proposed in the *Principles of the rights of patients in Europe*. One possible approach is to enact a framework law according to which provinces or regions should further elaborate patients' rights, while the framework law itself states that the patient should be informed on what those rights would be. Others are self-regulation, such as a patients' charter or a model contract concluded between organizations of physicians and of patients.

- Whether there should be national legislation on patients' rights to give effect to the principles, or whether other forms of regulation can serve the same purpose, depends on the national situation, legal culture and traditions.

- There will be national variations in what is laid down in regulations. Some particular aspect of patients' rights, such as the timing of access to services, might be of importance in a country and could be specifically included as a regulation.

- Some principles might be more difficult to implement in hospital than in other settings, because of the organizational constraints, the different roles of management and health care professionals, or even the problems of old buildings when it comes to such rights as territorial privacy.

- There could well be differences in the means of implementation between social rights and individual rights; for instance, in the field of collective or social rights (availability or financial accessibility of care) there is a more prominent role and responsibility for government.

Education and Information for Promoting Patients' Rights

- An explanatory memorandum elaborating on the principles of patients' rights would be very helpful to facilitate the greatest possible use of the WHO document within countries. It should also give guidance on the responsibilities of the main actors (governments, providers' organizations, patients' organizations and others) for the implementation of the principles.

- Reference needs to be made to the responsibilities of patients in addition to their rights. To avert the risk of a defensive reaction, for instance, from the medical profession, it is important to present the promotion of patients' rights as a common endeavour of all parties involved.

- Education of the population on health matters is needed, starting early in school. Such health education should also include patients' rights. The media also have a role in this respect.

- For health professionals, training on patients' rights is essential and should form part of the regular curriculum.

- Patients' organizations (either general or disease-specific ones) have an important role to play in the education of patients (to be distinguished from the education of citizens) and can contribute to the organization of such education.

Cooperative Strategies for Promoting Patients' Rights

- Patients' rights can and should be further developed through dialogue between the main actors, all of whom have responsibility for this development.

- Patients' organizations have a crucial role in this process, and should be represented at all different levels.

- The work of patients' organizations should be facilitated and endorsed by the authorities and, if need be, given financial support.

- There are problems in some countries in this field, however, such as the nonexistence of general patients' organizations. Where necessary, the government should stimulate the creation of a general patients' organization as a partner or counterpart for organizations of professionals at the national level.

- Organizations of health care professionals, hospitals and other provider institutions should not only develop codes of conduct but also see to their enforcement; they have an important role in trying to clarify the duties of their members *vis à vis* patients' rights and to seek ways to secure their application and to change attitudes among their members.

- Complaints procedures and a system of patient advocacy are important to enforcement of patients' rights and ensuring that patients in situations of conflict with providers receive advice and support.

Role of WHO and Other International Organizations

- WHO has responsibility for the continuing mass dissemination of the *Principles of the rights of patients in Europe* as a stimulus and backing for developments at the national level.

- There should be a follow-up mechanism to monitor and, after some years to assess countries' achievements in implementing the principles of patients' rights.

- WHO has a role in training, for example, the development of materials, and in advocacy, for example, ensuring that patients' rights are taken up as an issue in other present or future relevant WHO programmes and activities.

- The patient/consumer perspective should be taken into account in international consultations; international organizations should see to it that patients are represented, not just incidentally, but systematically and in an appropriate way.

- Other international organizations, including the World Medical Association and other nongovernmental organizations, should be sent the *Principles of the rights of patients in Europe*, so that they may take it into account when drawing up future guidelines or statements.

- Patients' rights and the implementation of the WHO principles should be an issue for closer interorganizational cooperation between the WHO European Regional Organization, the Council of Europe and the European Union.

15

Strategy for the Promotion of the Rights of Patients

H. Scicluna

According to the programme, I am invited to speak on the strategy for the promotion of the rights of patients. More modestly and as representing the Council of Europe, I will develop my conception of what the strategy could be at the international level.

I would like to start with a provocation. Personally, I dislike charters and lists of principles for two reasons. First, they are always presented as something complete, and they rarely are. There is always some right or other that is left out. Secondly, they are normally drafted in very general terms, in a way that everybody agrees with them, because they avoid the concrete application of what they should imply.

I may give two examples. Everybody agrees that a pregnant woman in trouble should be taken to hospital and taken care of. The trouble starts when the doctor, for reasons of conscience, refuses to carry out the abortion that is indicated. Everybody agrees that an elderly person who is ill should be taken to hospital when this is indicated, to be taken care of. The trouble starts when an elderly man, who is going to die within the next few weeks or months, is left to suffer until he dies. The problem starts when the reality of patients' rights is tested.

WHO (eds.), Promotion of the Rights of Patients in Europe, 127-130.

In the European Convention for the Protection of Human Rights and Fundamental Freedoms, there are no less than five articles that establish a right, but the Convention then proceeds to say that for several reasons, amongst them the protection of public health, those rights are diminished or suspended. There is Article 5 on the liberty and security, Article 8 on the right to private life, Article 9 on the right to freedom of thought, Article 10 on the right to freedom of expression, Article 11 on the right to freedom of peaceful assembly. All these rights are subject to this exception, and that is where possible abuses can arise, where the rights start operating in practice.

I should therefore make it clear that this does not mean that, as far as I am concerned, the list of principles that has been drawn up and presented here is useless. I think that the *Principles of the rights of patients in Europe* can be a very useful document, as long as we refrain from seeing it as some sort of papal encyclical that lays down infallible rules. We must see it as a practical tool for implementing the rights of patients in concrete situations. It is a tool to be used to increase the awareness of the public, the professionals and the patients themselves. It is not an end itself, not merely a contribution to the literature, but the beginning of a strategy to put into practice the principles that are contained in it.

So, what is the role of the Council of Europe in all this and why should it be interested? The fact is that that list of principles is intimately linked to two conventions, not just recommendations, but binding conventions, of the Council of Europe. The first is the human rights convention. I have already listed articles that actually mention public health and the protection of public health. The second convention is the European Social Charter, which has one article that grants the social right to the effective exercise of the right to health care.

Now, many of the articles in the *Principles of the rights of patients in Europe* are in fact covered by the human rights convention, and there have been several cases brought to the Court of Human Rights dealing with questions concerning health matters. I will mention just two cases. The first one, dating back to 1979, is Winterwerp versus the Netherlands, in which criteria were laid down by the Court on detention in psychiatric hospitals. The second case is van der Leer versus the Netherlands, in which it was held that a psychiatric detainee has to be informed beforehand that he or she is to be detained and why. As I have said, there is a very intimate link between the list of principles that have been drawn up and the human rights convention.

Another reason for the Council's interest is that we have never actually dealt with patients' rights as such. In 1985 there was a recommendation, but it was never adopted. It had been prepared and reached practically the final stages. It dealt with the obligation of doctors *vis à vis* patients. I cannot say whether the text that we have before us today was inspired by it, because I do not know whether the people who drafted it were aware of our recommendation. But it follows to a very large extent the principles that had been laid down in this 1985 draft document. Apart from that, we have dealt with patients' rights in several texts, but dealing with specific, concrete situations.

I will give a short list, drawn from a long list, of subjects that have been dealt with, on which there are already texts available: artificial procreation, organ transplant, genetic testing and screening, experimentation on humans, the ethics of blood transfusion, family planning, child abuse, ethical aspects of screening, ethical problems concerning the sick and the dying, ethical aspects of AIDS, internment of the mentally ill and the protection of medical data. In some cases, there is even a convention. This is the case with data. So I think that we could rightly say this is a subject that is of great interest to the Council of Europe. I should mention that, for next year, we are planning a whole series of activities dealing with discrimination and health, starting with the problems of discrimination in the case of employment and insurance.

In the light of this, how do we in the Council of Europe, with the interests that I have indicated, perceive this international strategy that I would like to see developed? I would like to make three points. First, we all agree that this is an extremely important subject. We might not all agree on the wording of every principle, but we all agree this is an important subject of major interest to all organizations dealing with health. Today, no organization that deals with health can afford to avoid the ethical dimension. Although I do not want to speak in their name, I can very well imagine that the European Union, now that it has a specific mandate on health, will be interested – in fact, I think it should be interested – in this ethical dimension.

Second, for some time now, there has been a new feeling of increased partnership between the European organizations. It has been a very interesting development, which started at various levels, but which now has reached the level of governmental interest, and therefore reached a stage at which the activities of the various organizations are better coordinated to avoid duplication and waste of money, energy and other resources. I think this increased sense of partnership is an important element.

Third, there is the role of the Council of Europe. It is not for me to sing our praises, but after what I have said, I think it is clear that it is not the case that we have a role in this particular strategy; we have a clear and particular role. In that role the most important thing that we want to achieve is the implementation of these principles in the various concrete situations in which they can and should be applied.

I believe that the first step should be that the two organizations that are mainly concerned, WHO and the Council of Europe, should be in contact with each other. WHO has launched this initiative. Perhaps it should now take a second initiative to start discussion with the Council of Europe on three objectives. First, a stock taking is needed. It is very important to find out exactly what has been done, to establish the state of the art today at the international level. The second objective is to determine priorities. Let us not make the mistake to which all international organizations are liable: to consider everything important and then to try to do everything. Even in a case like this, amongst these principles, there is undoubtedly, at a given time, one priority more urgent and important than others. The third objective is to decide on the activities that have to be done.

Having fulfilled those three objectives, we can then look at these activities and decide which activities the two organizations can do separately and together. That is a simple practical question of sharing activities. But – I repeat – there must first be the joint agenda setting of taking stock, of determining the priorities, and deciding on what the activities are to be. Then, the sharing of tasks can take place.

These are the views that I wanted to express. I should finish by saying that we have always, but particularly during the last few years, been working in a wonderful atmosphere and climate together with WHO, and I hope that this will be the opportunity even to improve on this relationship, if that were possible.

16

Chairman's Closing Address

W.H. Cense

We have been together to discuss one of the most important issues in health care, the rights of the patient. Increased awareness that the patient has a central position in health care, has stimulated the development of patients' rights. There is also a simultaneous development of social as well as individual rights in this field. The social dimension of patients' rights includes public health in its broadest sense, and rights to treatment and care, to adequate social cover and to benefit from progress in the field of health. There is now an urgent need for clarification and implementation of patients' rights.

We were here because it was felt time to strengthen the already observable trends and developments in Europe. This European Consultation was intended to contribute to the enhanced understanding and acceptance of patients' rights. It was called to define principles and strategies for the promotion of the rights of the patient within the context of health care system reforms. Various issues relating to patients' rights and various possibilities in their application at the different levels have been highlighted and explored in our discussions. My task now is to summarize on your behalf the main themes and to offer my assessment of what we have achieved.

As I have indicated, promoting and protecting the rights of the patient have two dimensions. One is the need to protect basic, individual, human rights; the other, the responsibility of government to assure a just and fair

WHO (eds.), Promotion of the Rights of Patients in Europe, 131-134.

health care system as a social right. Both aspects have been included in the set of principles of the rights of the patient, which has been presented to you by Professor Leenen and his colleagues The most important rights we have been discussing are those on information and consent, on privacy and confidentiality, and on care and treatment. Naturally the various rights require a different manner of implementation. Moreover, the actual implementation of these rights within a country depends heavily on its legislative or regulatory style and cultural diversity. We have been discussing these rights from the perspective of day-to-day patient care. We should also recognize that the individual rights to physical integrity and to privacy still apply after death, for instance, in the cases of organ removal and of medical research.

Patients' rights have implications for health professionals. Although retaining professional autonomy, the physician shares responsibility with the patient. In essence, the doctor–patient relationship is one of trust. Mutual trust is also a prerequisite for quality of care. Users of health care should be viewed as active partners of the treating doctor. This implies an end to traditional paternalistic attitudes. There has also been reference to the responsibility of the patient. Everybody will accept that, in order to behave responsibly, the patient should be enabled to behave responsibly. Hence the need for proper information, so the patient can take decisions and participate in the treatment process. Improvement in the quality of the doctor–patient relationship is part of a more general movement towards improving quality of care in general. There is no quality of care if the rights of the patient are not respected. Quality of care is enhanced through respect of patients' rights.

Patients' organizations have important responsibilities not only in the field of patient education and in discussions on health care services but also to promote the rights of the patient. They could, for instance, develop standards for the implementation of various patients' rights in close cooperation with the medical profession. It goes without saying that a partnership between patients' organizations and health care providers is needed if patients' rights are to be accepted and respected. Only through an open dialogue can a defensive reaction from the medical profession be avoided. For their part, health care professionals should be aware that the more they respect patients' rights, the less the risk of litigation.

Patients' organizations cannot function properly if they do not receive financial support. There are usually no financial problems for organizations of health care providers. It is one of the responsibilities of governments to ensure that there are none for patients' organizations. The respective positions should be in balance. Also, the possibility of patients' organizations that function at a European level should be considered.

Another issue that became evident was the need for education and training, both of health care personnel and of citizens. Education and information for the public at large contribute to achieving a better level of health, improving quality of care, as well as to the implementation of rights of the patient. Information on the legal position of the patient should be routinely included in the medical curriculum. The medical student should be taught how to communicate effectively with and be understood by the patient.

The international study by Leenen, Gevers and Pinet on the rights of patients in Europe,[1] led to the formulation of the document *Principles of the rights of patients in Europe* (see Chapter 4), which provides us with a European platform that corresponds to the common values to which European countries adhere. At the national level, such a set of principles provides an incentive and a point of reference when developing strategies for implementing patients' rights. Internationally, there is need for further cooperation and assistance. Because the rights of patients are of concern to various other international organizations, WHO should take the initiative to put the subject on the agenda of a common forum of WHO, the Council of Europe and the European Union, in the frame of the *rapprochement* between these organizations. It goes without saying that a duplication of activities by various international organizations does not serve the interest of the patient. Each organization should take up activities in this field for which it is best suited. Sometimes combined action might be necessary.

Ladies and gentlemen, I would like to thank you all for your very valuable contributions to our discussions. The results of this meeting deserve to be widely disseminated, and its recommendations implemented throughout Europe. It is an important achievement that we now have a set of principles to be used for the promotion and implementation of the rights of patients in WHO Member States. We have reached a very important stage in the promotion and protection of patients' rights in Europe. But it is not enough. There should now be an effort in all countries at the national, regional and local levels, to which you all can usefully contribute. You all go home now, I hope, with fresh ideas for promoting the rights of the patient

[1] LEENAN, H. ET AL. *The rights of patients in Europe.* Deventer, Kluwer Law and Taxation Publishers, 1993.

in your own surroundings. All of us should attempt to create a climate that is receptive for the promotion and protection of the rights of the patient.

17

Future Developments

Constantino Sakellarides

Patients' Rights In Europe

One of the prevailing ideas in the discussions held during the European Consultation on Rights of the Patient was that patients' rights are an essential element of an appropriate health care partnership between patients, health care providers and health care managers. It is indeed important that the different approaches adopted to promote patients' rights – declarations of principles, charters for concrete action, legal requirements or others – are seen as ways to enhance citizens' and patients' entitlement to a real health care partnership.

Sustaining this partnership is a continual and very demanding process. A very distinguished European, Jean-Jacques Rousseau, wrote in his *Social contract* that, if there were a people of gods, they would choose the ways of democracy to rule their conduct, but he also added that, for simple humans such as ourselves, that was really much more difficult. It takes persistent, relentless effort and alertness at all times to develop, promote and maintain the spirit and practice of partnership.

Patient rights in Europe have been more forcefully pursued over the last few years and we were able to prepare and adopt A Declaration on the Promotion of Patients' Rights because so many of those present in this Consultation have shown such sustained interest and enduring commitment to patients' rights.

WHO (eds.), Promotion of the Rights of Patients in Europe, 135-139.

Preparing the Declaration

The adoption of this Declaration came as a result of a long and quite elaborate preparatory process. An important landmark in this process was a European survey on patients' rights that was conducted and analysed by an international study group supported by WHO. This study[1] has been a useful background document in our discussions.

A second and very significant initiative in this process was the preparation a discussion document *Principles of the rights of patients in Europe*, which was drafted by a group of international experts and was submitted for broad consultation with governments and other institutions in European countries.

This document has been now incorporated in the Declaration and therefore adopted as a European reference for developing more country-specific declarations or charters on patients' rights throughout Europe.

This Consultation has been made possible by the strong support of the Government of the Netherlands, particularly through the very committed involvement of Dr Van Etten and Dr Winberg.

This illustrates well the fact that the Amsterdam Declaration is indeed the culmination of a process of fact finding and analysis, strategic thinking and design, broad consultation and participation, extensive debate and the appropriate exercise of health leadership.

But let us now look ahead.

Promoting the Amsterdam Declaration

The first type of initiative will be to find very practical means for the wide dissemination of this Declaration. This can be done immediately. Then it is important to pull together the different technical contributions that have been prepared, presented and discussed in this Consultation and make them available as an accessible technical publication. This will provide to all

---

[1] LEENEN, H. ET AL., *The rights of patients in Europe*. Deventer, Kluwer Law and Taxation Publishers, 1993.

interested parties a substantive reference document on the main issues related to patients' rights and will therefore complement and support the appropriate use of the Declaration.

During the Consultation, leading health officials from more than one country have manifested keen interest in promoting a first encounter of the key interested parties in patients' rights to discuss the Amsterdam Declaration and devise effective strategies to promote patients' rights. Some countries may require some degree of international support in designing and implementing these strategies.

WHO will make a special effort to integrate the principles of this Declaration into its different programmes and to use these more forcefully to promote patients' rights in Europe. This certainly applies to WHO initiatives on health care reform, hospital care and primary health care, nursing and general practice. This is a very relevant issue to bring more often into the agenda of the European Forum of Medical Associations. The supportive presence of the current Chairman of the Forum in the Consultation is certainly encouraging in this regard. There are other areas of WHO's programme of work where patients' rights are particularly relevant. These include programmes related to specific population groups that tend to see their rights weakened by tradition, as in the case of women, by social exclusion, as in the case of migrant populations, the unemployed and the poor, or because they suffer from a particular disease or conditions, such as drug and alcohol abuse or AIDS.

In this regard the European health policy conference, which took place in Copenhagen in December 1994, will provide an opportunity to disseminate the Declaration and to look at patients' rights from a broader health policy perspective and bring a stronger view of patients' rights into the European health for all strategy.

The participation of the Council of Europe in this Consultation was particularly important for the patients' rights movement. It is well known that the Council of Europe plays a highly significant role in the promotion of the principles of democracy and human rights in Europe. It is therefore clear that the Council of Europe will continue to pay special attention to patients' rights and we are sure that the close cooperation between the Council and WHO in these and other areas will continue. The need to invite into such cooperation some of the relevant departments of the European

Commission was very much stressed during the Consultation. This also applies to a number of nongovernmental organizations that are very active in this area.

Monitoring Progress in Patients' Rights

If we are indeed serious in promoting patients' rights in Europe, then we need closely to monitor our achievements and failures and to learn from them. It is necessary to develop a simple but effective mechanism to follow up on the Amsterdam Declaration, to find out what is happening, to measure its impact, to recognize and share successes among interested parties, and to recognize and try to settle problems. For that purpose, we need to identify and introduce in our information and display systems a selected number of indicators and analytical summaries that would allow this monitoring function.

We hope to be able to report some progress in this monitoring system at the European conference on health care in transition, to be held in Ljubljana in June 1996.

An Open Mind for Change

WHO understands this Declaration to be a very important tool to further patients' rights in Europe. But we see this as a very dynamic process.

Life is movement. New ideas are emerging, there are organizational, managerial and clinical innovations in health care everywhere. We have to be flexible, well informed and intellectually robust to be able to incorporate these innovations into our thinking.

We may need to introduce more forcefully into the patients' rights movement the concepts of effective health care, and that of quality development as it relates to the improvement of health care outcomes.

It could be desirable to address patients' rights in the broader context of citizens' voice and choice and to look at their implications for social and health policy.

Finally, it might be useful to integrate into the same policy framework patients' rights and responsibilities. This would emphasize the reciprocal obligations of the key partners of the health care process.